GARDEN OF LOVE

ALAN HINES

Order this book online at www.trafford.com
or email orders@trafford.com

Most Trafford titles are also available at major online book retailers.

Print information available on the last page.

ISBN: 978-1-4907-9741-0 (sc)
ISBN: 978-1-4907-9740-3 (e)

Trafford rev. 09/13/2019

 www.trafford.com
North America & international
toll-free: 1 888 232 4444 (USA & Canada)
fax: 812 355 4082

Acknowledgements: Thank you Heavenly Father for blessing me to live to see yet another day. Thank you for constantly casting blessings my way. Thank you for even putting on my heart to become a book writer.....Thanks to my mom and grandmother may they both rest in peace.....Thanks to everybody that showed my any type of love in life.....Thanks to everyone that support me as an author.

BOOKS OF POETRY ALREADY PUBLISHED BY ALAN HINES,

1. Reflections of Love
2. Thug Poetry Volume 1
3. The Words I Spoke
4. Joyce
5. Constant Visions
6. Red Ink of Blood
7. Beauty of Love
8. Reflections of Love Volume 2
9. Reflections of Love Volume 3
10. True Love Poetry
11. Visionary.
12. Love Volume 1
13. This is Love

URBAN NOVEL ALREADY PUBLISHED BY ALAN HINES,

1. Book Writer
2. Queen of Queens

UPCOMING BOOKS OF POETRY BY ALAN HINES,

1. Reflections of Love (Volume 2, and 3)
2. This is Love (Volume 1, 2, and 3)
3. Founded Love (Volume 1,2, and 3)
4. True Love (Volume 1,2, and 3)
5. Love (Endless Volumes)
6. Tormented Tears (Volume 1,2, and 3)
7. A Inner Soul That Cried (Volume 1,2, and 3)
8. Visionary (Endless Volumes)
9. A Seed That Grew (Volume 1,2, and, 3)
10. The Words I Spoke (Volume 2, and 3)
11. Scriptures (Volume 1,2, and 3)
12. Revelations (volume 1,2, and 3)
13. Destiny (Volume 1,2, and 3)
14. Trials and Tribulations (Volume 1,2, and 3)
15. IMMORTALITY (Volume 1,2, and 3)

16. My Low Spoken Words (Volume 1,2, and 3)
17. Beauty Within (Volume 1,2, and 3)
18. Red Ink of Blood (Volume 1,2, and 3)
19. Destiny of Light (Jean Hines) (Volume 1,2, and 3)
20. Deep Within (Volume 1, 2, and 3)
21. Literature (Volume 1, 2, and 3)
22. Silent Mind (Volume 1,2, and 3)
23. Amor (Volume 1,2, and 3)
24. Joyce (Volume 1,2, and 3)
25. Lovely Joyce (Volume 1,2, and 3)
26. Pink Lady (Volume 1,2, and 3)
27. Mockingbird Lady (Volume 1,2, and 3)
28. Godly tendicies (Volume 1,2, and 3)
29. Enchanting Arrays (Volume 1,2, and 3)
30. Harmony (Volume 1,2, and 3)
31. Realism (Volume 1,2, and 3)
32. Manifested Deep Thoughts (Volume 1,2, and 3)
33. Poectic Lines of Scrimage (Volume 1,2, and 3)
34. Garden of Love (Volume 1,2, and 3)
35. Reflection In The Mirror. (Volume 1,2, and 3)

UPCOMING NON-FICTION BOOKS BY ALAN HINES,

1. Time Versus Life
2. Timeless Jewels
3. The Essence of Time
4. Memoirs of My Life
5. In my Eyes To See
6. A Prisoner's Black History

UPCOMING URBAN NOVELS BY ALAN HINES,

1. Black Kings
2. Playerlistic
3. The Police
4. Scandalous
5. The West Side Rapist
6. Shattered Dreams

1. SPRINGTIME

We will spend each day in the time of
spring, Martin Luther after God
and Jesus all hail to the new born king, living out dreams.
Love, life, and reality as it seems.
Honoring the love of God as we sail down streams.
Crowned, ordained as my queen.
Loyalty as a must, everything.
The love of vitality, living out dreams.
Love of life in which it seems.

2. ALTHOUGH

Although you are far away everyday on my knees I pray.
Lovely as a new born on a summer's day.
Although you are far away,
thou shall not go astray.
And every minute you gone I miss you more day by day.
Far away love shall never fade.
Although far away, my heart is with you love shall remain to stay.

3. BEAUTY WITHIN

Although she had light brown smooth skin
hazel eyes of a cat descendants; she was more
beautiful within.
She'd listen to me talk with no end.
She was my best of best friend.
She was religious, a life without sin.
No phonyness to contend, or bend.
Her heart was built to show love to
women and men.
She studied religious books with no end.
She was a saint and prophet within,
mixed as beautiful blend.
She liked my poetry as if it made her feel
the cool breeze of wind, happy days with no
end, mentally in the air she'd suspend.
She wanted to hear my poetry again,
and again.
She liked to square dance, and romance.
She made everyone come together as friends.
Because of her writers utilized their pens
to create romantic poetry that made love extend.....
Beauty Within.

4. Part Of My Silent Mind

She became a part of my silent mind.
She was one of the reason why I started to rhyme.
Made the sun shine.
Took me to places hard to find.

She had a personality that was of another time.
Biblical divine.

Opening my eyes to the things that I was once blind.

She help me get through troublesome times.
Gave me a piece of mind.
A light that shine.

Without me saying it she knew my pain,
she knew my love, she knew my shine.....

Part of my silent mind.

5. FORTUNATE

Fortune and fame.
Plain as Jane.
Unique dame.
Eases brain.
Infinite fortunate fame.
For you I'll never change.
Poetry became.
Love to obtain,
fortune and fame.

6. I'LL BRING LOVE

I'll bring love instead of pain.
Wild animals to tame.
Pleasure you'll gain.
Happiness to come, again.
A trophy to frame.
Love gained.

7. I Wanna Be You

I wanna be you.
Love coming true.
Love due.
For you be the reason I feel brand new.
I wanna be you.

8. ROMANCE STORY

Story consist of love.
Titled romance of love it is,
it was.
Heaven's above.
Encouraging other's to spread love.
Romance and love.

9. BROUGHT LIGHT

To light as sky rockets in flight.
Gave dead new life.
To light imagination of visions
in clear view of sight.
In life she brought things to light.

10. EMOTIONS

Emotions came out.
Love beyond a reasonable doubt.
I glorify your name from my mouth.
Emotions that have clout.

11. THE BEST

You are the best.
Never settle for less,
and be blessed.

12. ENLIGHT

Enlights the world.
Special lady, special girl.
Rainbows with swirls.
Planted seeds fertile.
The element that lights the world.

13. THANKS FOR MOMENTS IN TIME

Thanks for moments in time.
A reason a rhyme.
Poetic grind.
16 bars poetic lines.
Love the way you shine.
Love having you as mines.
Love the trees, the mountains,
and the vines we climb.
Love having you all the time.
Love the way you shine.
Love making you rhyme.

14. GLORIA

A historian.
Told glorious stories.
Stress free no worries.
Beautiful days, no thunder storms, no rain
or flurries.....
Gloria.

15. PLEASE LOVE

Your presence.
A princess.
Tender caress.
Lover and a friend.
Love from the beginning to the end.

16. CONTROLLED MINDS

Controlled minds.
Love all the time.
The light that shined.
Contolled love within the essence of time.

17. POSTERITY

Keys to posterity.
Unique.
Love being reached.
A leader to teach.
To my ears music to me.
Love is all I see.
Posterity.

18. EVIDENT

Time well spent.
Love that was meant.
Spiritually inclined,
and evident.

19. GREATEST LADY

Greatest lady ever.
Love didn't get any better.

Greatest of all times.
Love making love to minds.

Greatest one I ever met.
Mutual love no regret.

20. A WONDERFUL

A wonderful life to live.
Wonderful love to give.
Wonderful she is.

21. THE TREE

The tree of knowledge.
The tree of growth.
The tree of love.
The tree of the spiritual
holy ghost.

22. LOVELY SHE

Lovely she as colors
of brightness be.

Lovely she as the Mermaids
that swim through the Sea.

Lovely she my lady of love to forever be.

23. FOREVER BE

Forever be mines.
Forever shine.
Forever remain in your prime.

24. HOMAGE

The days of homage.
Positive graduates of college.
Being marvelous.
Honoring God regardless.

25. SHINE BRIGHT

Shine bright.
Great sense of delight.
Reaching great heights.

26. BEFORE AND AFTER

Before and after.
Honored God's word before the rapture.

Before and after,
love she'd mastered.

Before and after,
love came unconceiled,
it came to be ravishing.

27. LOVE ORDAINED

Love ordained.
Love gained.
Love simply hearing her name.

28. MY EVERYTHING

My everything.
My queen of queens.
Such a delighful human being.
My love in it's entirety, everything.

29. FOR HER

For her I'll give all the love in store.

For her I'll travel many miles to see.

For her I'll be all I can be.

30. GALORE, ADORE

Galore.
Adore.
Your love always wanting more.

31. SHE KEEP

She keep me on my toes, my feet.
Love in it's entirety complete.
Love that was free.

32. IF I WAS BIRD

If I was bird,
I'd spread my wings of love to be.
I'd soar through the sky ambitious
be a visionary to see.

If I was bird I'd fly high
as a way of love to be free.

If I was a bird I'd fly many miles
for my love to see.

If I was a bird I'd fly free.

33. GIVE ME

Give me a piece of mind.
A light that shine.
The spring and summer time.
Love that's divine.

34. AND THE JOY

And the joy you bring.
Glorify and sing.
All hail to the newborn queen.

35. SPACE AND TIME

Space and time.
Love of mines.
Lovely and kind.
Pleasant and fine.
Love throughout the space
of lifetime.

36. TRANSFORMATION

A duckling to a swan.
A caterpillar to a butterfly.
Love above and beyond the clouded skies.

37. FOREVER LOVE

Love to live forever, eternal ties.
Love without be capable of demise.
Love a blessing, uprise.

38. GAVE SHE

She gave me hope.
She gave me love.
She gave peace,
just because.
She gave me a new life,
she gave be hers.

39. MINES

Love of mines.
Forever in time.
Lovely and divine.
Love the way she made me glow
to shine.

40. GREW

Grew like a planted seed of fruit.
Grew like the timeless essence of love due.
Grew tall as the skies, blue.
Cool breeze in the summer time, blew.
Melodies of a flute.
Love due.....
The pleasure of the love that grew.

41. IN LOVE

In love with who she is,
who she was.

In love with the greatness
of her just because.

In love with her love that floods.

42. IN TIME

In time love shall prevail.
In time love shall free to exhale.
In time love shall be all as well.

43. Naturally Giving

Naturally giving.
Love of life living.
The caress of love as a beautiful feeling.

44. SHE GAVE

She gave me love.
She gave me life.
As the other way around poetry
for me she'd right.

She gave me hope.
She gave me sight.
She love in the days turned to night.

45. LOVELY

Lovely as can be.
Lovely she.
Lovely and free.

46. LOVE BEYOND

Love beyond the clouded skies.
Love beyond eternal no demise.
Love beyond, but free as enterprise.

47. LIFE, AND LOVE

My life, my love.
My will, she was.

My life, my love.
My freedom thereof.

My life, my love.
My guardian angel from up above.

48. LOVERS LANE

Lovers lane.
Lovers we became.
Love that was gain.

49. LOVE, TIME

Rhythm and ryhme.
The essence of time.
Making love to minds.
Love at it's best kind.
Love that will last throughout time.

50. EASY AND FREE

Easy and free.
Lovely as can be.
Wonderful to me.
Easy and free.

51. I Feel Her

I feel her spirit,
I feel her soul.
I feel her as harvest to grow.
I feel her love as a melody, a tempo.
I feel her love as a grip that I never want to let go.
I feel her love, her spirit, her soul.

52. SPREAD LOVE

Spread love like wings of an Eagle.
Living as a sequel.
Treating everyone as a equal.

Spread love like wings of an Eagle.

53. EVERLASTING

Forever,
everlasting.
Love gonna last,
everlasting.
Forever casting.
Love everlasting.

54. Such A

Such a divine woman,
love in abundance.

Such a wonderful lady,
wonderful woman.

Such a precious lady,
stunning and cunning.

55. GRACE

Grace.
Can't be replace.
Love that was laced.
Will, might, and grace.

56. HE CRAVED

He craved for her mind,
knowledge, wisdom and understanding so he wont be left behind.

He craved for her soul to be together as they grow old.

57. LOVE CONTEND

It begin with no end.
Love to contend.
A lover a friend.
She was God's gift to me,
a blessed man.

58. CRAVED

He craved for her night, and day to him she was like a better
movement, a better way.

He dreamed of her with no end.
A lover and friend.

He craved her mind, body, soul.
Her craved her to be as a red Rose
to blossom to grow.

59. LOVE CAME

Love came.
Love gain.
Glorify thou name.

60. IN TIME

In time, shine.
In time make love to minds.
In time be the best of all times.

61. GOD'S CHILD

She made love last forever in it's while.
Enhanced smiles.
Godly God's child.

62. Love and Romance

Love and romance.
Changing circumstance.
Affection to enhance.

63. SHE WAS

She was the light the day.
Everyday to god in Jesus name
she'll pray.

She was my everyday Valentine,
love of a lifetime.

She was my way of being freed, free.
For i am her she is me.

64. ENABLED

Enabled me to live.
Enabled me to love throughout years.
Enabled me to be blessed performing
in which was sincere.

65. A LOVELY

A lovely shine.
This lovely light of mines.
This love of a lifetime.

66. WITHIN

Within heart and mind
love incliined.

Within livilyhood and
vitality love became reality.

Within space and time she made
love to my mind.....

67. TO BE

Love to be.
Love that was free.
My truest love
within a straight
path for only me to see.

68. WAS

Was that of another time,
lovely and divine.

Was a great like the lakes,
I never wanted to escape.

Was a a gift a treasure,
love didn't get any better.

69. MY GAIN

Substain.
Gained.
Love a peace multiplied,
my everything.

70. RIGHTEOUS

Righteous.
Uplifting,
uprighting.
Lovely sightings.
Delighting.

71. ENGRAVED

Engraved.
spiritual, far from man made.
Beautiful array.
Cherish the life,
cherish the day.

Love in my heart engraved.

72. LOVE IN HEART

Love in my heart.
Shining in the dark.
A rest haven amongst the stars.
The greatest joy of love thus far.

73. In Her I Seen

In her I seen the light.
In her I seen power, love, destiny, sight.
In her I seen a new life.

74. IT BECAME

It became wonderful lovely, love.
It became the grace of love.
It became the everlasting love to flood.

75. PART

Part of my silent mind.
Love and tranquility combine.
It became part of my silent mind
I'd think of you all the time.
It became part of my silent mind,
the love my life, the love of a lifetime.

76. CREATED

Created peace within.
Lover and a friend.

Created a way in giving,
freed me from a system of trapped prism.

Created a signs of times.
Holy and divine.

77. MY LIGHT, MY ROCK

My light, my rock.
Love non stop.

My freedom, my will.
Love until.

My craft, my pleasure.
Love forever.

78. In Time Shine

In time shine.
Be great all the time.
Make love to minds.
Be as the scriptures say,
holy, divine.

79. FOREVER

Forever live,
forever give.

Forever be,
forever see.

Forever and a day.
Love to stay.

80. OF LIFE

Days of life.
Periodic paradise.
Love twice as nice.

81. MY LOVE

My love she was.
My love she is.
My love I'll create no tears.
My love lets remain together until
the ending of life years.
My love she is.

82. APPLE

An apple of seeded knowledge,
growth, prosperity, marvelous.

An apple the fruit for thought love sought.

An apple of giving love, my angel from above.

83. PLEASE

Pleased by love to suceed.
Inner feelings emotions came forth freed.
Pleased by your love indeed.
Pleased in the way your treat others,
the way you treat me.

84. CAN

Can and will.
Love to feel.
Love that was real.

85. WONDERFUL, FANTASTIC

Wonderful, fantastic.
Loving above average.
Wonderful, lavish.
Fantastic, above average,
lavish.

86. Everytime

Everytime you cross my mind,
love shines.

Everytime I simply hear your name,
a smile is gain.

Everytime I think of you I think of skies blue,
being near you, lovely love that's due.

87. SINCERE

Love sincere.
Love my dear.
Love having you here.

88. HARVEST OF LOVE

My life, my world.
My lady, my girl.
My diamond, my pearl.
My harvest of love to be fertile.

89. CONCEIVE

Conceive.
Love indeed.
Same air to breathe.
Nourishment of love to feed.

90. LOVE GAVE

Love gave.
Amazed.
Everglades.

91. EVER SO MORE

Ever so more.
The tenderness of loves core.
Always wanting more.

92. FOUND

Found a way.
Love to stay.
Love more each day.

93. SEASON

The on going changing seasons.
Love for a reason.
Love a pleasure pleasing.
Undying love without grieving.

94. IT CAME

It came from a planted vision.
Love in existence.
Love from near or a distance.
Love relentless.

95. FREEDOM OF

Freedom of speech, freedom of choice.
Freedom of love, freedom to voice.
Freedom to vibe, freedom to bring love alive.

96. In The Beginning

In the beginning with no end love begin.
In the beginning spiritual love to contend.
In the beginning love came free from sin.

97. DAYS

Lovely days.
Enchanting arrays.
Love was made.

98. HER SPIRIT

Her spirit I shall forever more feel it.
Her vibe kept the hope and opportunity alive.
Her love was cast from up above.

99. EASY AND FREE

Love sparks.
shining in the dark.
Easy and free from the start.

100. CARGO

Better days tomorrow.
Loving without sorrow.
A blessing that carry weight cargo.

Upcoming Urban Novel by Alan Hines

Scandalous

CHAPTER 1

As Prince's song Scandalous slightly echoed in the room at a low pleasant tone through the surround sound speakers, as he constantly inhaled and exhaled the blunt filled with loud, relaxing he could visualize good things to be, making more money, and growth and development in the drug game.

And then he heard a knock on the door.....

Fontane opened the door and there she stood there with a brown trench coat on. Such a radiant beauty looking like a Goddess on Earth.....

Before she could step all the way in the door, in her own silent mind she admired the aroma of the wonderful smell of the loud smoke, as it made her slightly begin to cough.....

"Step in, I wasn't expecting you for another hour or two," Fontane said. "My kids went to sleep early so I decided to come over while they was asleep. You promise you aren't going to tell anybody," she said. "Girl stop playing you know I aint gone tell nobody," Fontane said. "I'm not like these other ho's that's always out here selling pussy, I'm just doing this because my man locked up, and I got bills to pay," she said.....

Without saying another word she stood up off the couch dropped the trench coat, and there she stood as naked as the day she was born. The biggest roundest prettiest titties imaginable she possessed. The pussy so hairy looked like chinchilla fur. She turned around to show off her big ole ass.

His mouth dropped, and dick got so hard it felt like it was going to bust. He immediately took his clothes off. He wondered if he'd use a rubber or not, within seconds he made up his mind not to, he figured that if he was finna pay for the pussy he might as well get his money worth.....

As both of them was still standing he bent her over as she used her hands on the couch for stability, he forced his dick in her tight wet pussy, and begin fucking the shit out of her as if he was made at the world.....Within five pumps he nutted unloaded all of it in her guts. She was disappointed, and pleased at the same time that he nutted so fast; she was disappointed because it felt so wonderful and she wanted the pleasure to be endless, she was pleased because she knew her pussy was a bomb in which made him nut quick.....

"Bend down and suck this dick bitch," Fontane said. "Boy watch your mouth," she said in a low soft tone.....

with no hesitation she got on her knees with an aim to please, to her mouth was fantastic; she'd suck on the dick thoroughly, while strocking it with her right hand all at the same damn time.

In no time flat he was busting nuts down her throat; he couldn't believe it because it was hard for any chick to make him nut by sucking his dick.

He laid her on her back on the couch and begin squeezing and sucking her titties, as if he was breast feeding as she held her own legs up he begin giving her the dick in it's most harsh form as she continously begged for him to do it harder.....

For hours on and off they performed hardcore sex.....

As it was time to go she put on her high heels and trench coat as he stared, and watched admiring the view.....

"Okay nigga what's the hold up give me my four hundred," she said. "Here, here go six hundred whenever you need some financial assistance please let me know," Fontane said.

She snatched the money out his hand happy as a kid at Christmas time, as she waved at him, and told him bye.....

CHAPTER 2

Fontane begin to feel his phone vibrating. "Hello," Fontane said. "Hello can I speak to Fontane," Chresha said. "Yeah this me, who is this," Fontane asked? "This is Chresha." "Why do everytime you call me you always ask to speak to me, and you know you calling my phone, I mean do that make any sense to you," Fontane asked. "Because I knoe sometimes you be having other people answer your phone," Chresha said. "Girl you know aint nobody answering my phone," Fontane said. "Why do you always ask who this is calling you, what you got another girlfriend or something," Chresha said. "You know damn well I'm not fucking with nobody but you," Fontane said. "Good game, real phony," she said.....

"I've been missing you and shit lately, you must got another bitch because you don't spend no time with me," Chresha said. "You know me I've been traveling state to state doing business ventures," Fontane said. "Business ventures my ass, you been traveling state to state to buy dope," Chresha said. "Is you done lost your motherfucking mind, you can't be saying shit like that over the phone, the feds could have my phone tapped," Chresha said. "Nigga you aint on shit, the feds aint thinking about you, you aint moving enough product," Chresha said.....

Little did she know he was moving more than enough product for the Feds to be watching. His connect in Chicago was supplying him with enough dope to supply a third of Flint city.....

"I'm serious Chresha you gotta be careful of what you say over the phone cuz the Feds can popp a nigga ass for little petty shit they say over the phone. They'll have my ass way in the basement in the Feds joint across country, some motherfucking where," Fontane said.

"Well since you say I haven't been spending that much time with you, why don't you come over now, and wear one of them new lingerie sets under your clothes," Fontane said. "Which one you want me to wear," Chresha asked? "It don't matter just pick one of the newest ones," Fontane said. "A'ight I got you, I'm going to bring my sister with me," Chresha said. "For what," he asked with authority.....He hated her twin sister Teressa with a passion.

"I want to bring her over to do what you've been asking me to do," Chresha said. "What's that," he asked? "You know what you've been wanting me to do," Chresha said. "What's that," Fontane asked again? "The threesome," she respond.....

His mouth dropped as he dropped the phone on the floor.....

He picked up the phone and immediately asked, "are you serious." "Yeah I'm serious we wanna do it," Chresha said.

"You trying to tell me that as much as me and your sister can't stand each other she wants me to fuck her," he said. "Yes, that's exactly what I'm saying," she said.....

Fontane paused for a minute in disbelief, and overjoyed that he was going to have a threesome with two twin sisters.

"A'ight, ya'll come on over here and bring some drinks with ya'll," Fontane said.

He went into the room popped a Viagara he stole from his grandfather, and an x-pill, and then fired up a leaf joint. He rushed smoking his leaf joint; he was a closet leaf smoker he didn't want nobody to know he smoked leaf.....

Fontane sat back high as kite visualizing how beautiful the girls look; The twins looked just alike, short, thick ass hell, caramel complexion, smooth skin, dark brown eyes.....

In no time flat the girls were at his house; it seemed like they flew a private jet over there, because they came so fast.

The door bell ring twice; Fontane went to the door looked out his peep hole and to his surprise the girls were standing there. He thought to himself, like damn how they get over here that quick.

He immediately opened the door before he could say a word Chresha put her index finger to her lips to sush him.

As Chresha and Teressa entered his home, Chresha locked the door. Both women grabbed him by each one of his hands and led him into his bedroom.

Inside fontane felt like a kid again on the verge of it being his first time getting some pussy.

Within seconds both girls were in their birthday suits standing side by side each other, awaiting for him to undress and give out orders.

Fontane undressed and got on his knees on the bed; he ordered Chresha to suck his dick. Chresha got on the bed on all fours and begin sucking the shit out of his dick.

Teressa begin finger fucking Chresha ass and pussy with two fingers in each hole, right hand fingers in the pussy hole, left hand fingers in the asshole. Fontane couldn't believe what was taking place.

As Fontane was on the verge of busting a nut Teressa begin eating Chresha's pussy in which made his nut burst out like an erupting Volcano.

Fontane begin thinking to himself, these ho's done did this shit before; why they didn't been do this with me. These ho's some freaks doing insence, and everything.

Once Teressa completed eating Chresha out momentarily, Fontane told her to lay on the bed. She laid on the bed flat on her stomach as Fontane begin stuffing his dick in and out her pussy. Teressa laid on the bed watching them while sucking on the two fingers that she'd stuck in Chresha's ass while finger fucking herself with two fingers from her other hand.

Just when Fontane was getting ready to nut he told Teressa, "take your fingers outta your mouth and give me a kiss."

While Fontane and Teressa tongues entertwine she continued fingering herself as Fontane commence to stuff his dick into Chresha pussy.

Fontane then told Teressa to lay flat on her stomach as he begin to enter Teressa he could feel a big difference from Chresha; Teressa's pussy was much tighter, and moist. Now was has chance to take out all his anger, frustration, and dislike for Teressa on her pussy.

He shoved his dick in her with force, and commenced to fucking her like he was mad at the world. She pleaded for him to stop as he continued going, giving her the dick in it's rawest form.

Once he unloaded his sperm cells in her she jumped up yelling, "I told you to stop." He grabbed her head and begin tongue kissing her, the kiss kinda put her at ease.

After he finished kissing Teressa he started kissing Chresha. Then Chresha and Teressa begin kissing one another.....

As Fontane maintained his composure, deep down within he was going wild inside.....

For hours into the morning came around without to many intermissions they fucked and sucked one another.....

As the night turned into, reached morning all three sat watched the sun rise will listening to Jazz at a low tone. They laughed and talked reminiscing about last night making plans to do it again.

They ended up showering seperately as everybody went their seperate ways; but right before they left the house Fontane told them, "I'm a call ya'll later on." "Make sure you do," Chresha said.

He hugged both girls and they left, and went their seperate ways.

Fontane fired up a Newport Long and got on the phone to call his guy Rob.....

"Rob guess who I fucked last night," Fontane said. "Who is this," Rob asked? "This Fontane, guess who I fucked last night," Fontane said. "Who," Rob asked? "I fucked Chresha and Teressa together," Fontane said. "No you didn't, get your ass outta here," Rob said. "On my momma I fucked Chresha, and Teressa, and they fucked each other," Fontane said. "Straight up, did they," Rob said. "Yup," Fontane said. "How you pull that off you must of paid that," Rob said? "Naw I didn't pay, shiit I would've thou," Fontane said, as they both begin laughing.....

"I've been sweating Chresha to have a threesome with me and another woman for a long ass time. So yesterday she call me on some emotional shit talking about we aint been spending very much time together, and some other ole goofy ass shit she was talking about. So I told her to come on over to my crib. She tells me that her and Teressa wanted to do a threesome. At first I thought she was bullshitting because Teressa and me can't stand each other.

Come to find out she wasn't bullshitting. They came straight over and got to work. Them ho's done did that shit before," Fontane said. "When you gonna set them out to the guys," Rob asked? "Not yet later," Fontane said. "Why not know instead of later," Rob asked? "I already know how they is it's gonna take a while for them to do it with somebody else," Fontane said.....

Fontane was lying he didn't wanna set them out, he loved Chresha.

"A man I gotta go the cleaner's, I'll catch up with you later on," Fontane said. "A'ight man I holler at you, love nigga," Rob said. "Love," Fontane said.

Later on tha night Fontane cell phone rang.....

"Hello," Fontane said. "I thought you said you was gonna call us," Chresha said. "I got caught in some business deals, other than that I would've call," Fontane said. "Come over here tonight me and Teressa wanna see you, and spend some time with you," Chresha said. "I can't I'm in the middle of some business right now, other than that I'll be there; I promise Ill be over there tomorrow for sho," Fontane said. "I gotta work tomorrow," Chresha said. "Well I'll come over there after work, but before I hang up what made you, and Teressa wanna do that with me," Fontane asked? "I love you, and shit and I'll do anything for you," Teressa said.....

Fontane remained quiet for a seconds pleased with her answer made him feel like a player.....

"But what made Teressa wanna do that," Fontane asked? "She really like you," Chresha said. "Now you know damn well me and Teressa can't stand each other," Fontane said. "That's what you thought, she always liked you," Chresha said. "Be for real, Teressa is the only person I ever met that I argue with everytime we're around," Fontane said. "You just didn't know deep down inside, she liked you, and always wanted to give you some of that pussy," Chresha said.....

Fontane paused for the matter of seconds letting it mirinate in his head.....oh well fuck it if they wanna have threesomes who gives a fuck if she likes me or not, Fontane thought to himself.....

"But uhhh anyway tell Teressa I said, what's up," Fontane said. "A'ight," Chresha said. "I gotta go," Fontane said. "Promise you'll be over here tomorrow when you get off work," Chresha said. "I promise," Fontane said. "I love you," Chresha said. "A'ight i" ll holla," Fontane said as the both ended their call.....

The next day Fontane came over and picked up Teressa while Chresha was at work. He took her shopping spent five hundred on 2 pair of high heel shoes.....

Afterwards they went to the show. Once the movie was over they road around town ended up naked, sexing at a sleazy motel.....

Teressa, and Chresha lived together. Once he took Teressa home he had a long talk with her. "Teressa now you know what goes on between me and you stays between me and you," Fontane said. "What do you mean by that," Teressa asked? "Whatever we do when Teressa aint around is between you, and I," Fontane said. "You know damn well I aint no dummy, I aint gonna tell Teressa that we fucked and you took me shopping when she wasn't around, let me tell you a little secret," Teressa said. "What's that," Fontane asked? "I always liked your stanking ass," Teressa said. "You showl gotta a way with showing people you like them," Fontane said. "That's just the way I am, I'm snotty as hell; well anyway let's not bring up old shit," Teressa said.....

She begin to smile genuinely as if she was happy than she ever been in life.....

"You know me and my sister will do anything for you. Whatever we can do to make you happy we're all for it, seeing you happy will only make us more happier," Teressa said.....

He slowly move his face towards hers as their tongues collided, as he was trying to kiss her suck her lips and tongue all at once.

He then stood her up pulled her pants down to her knees. Then pulled his pants down to his knees, bent her over and gave her the dick hardcore in the rawest form.....

Afterwards they sat down and watched some midget porn until they dosed off and went to sleep.....

By the time Chresha came in from work Teressa, and Fontane were fully dressed sound asleep on the couch.....

Chresha walked through the door seen him on the couch and instantly began smiling.....

Chresha walked slowly over to him, dropped her purse took off all her clothes, and laid them on the floor.

She tapped him gently on his head..... "Wake up sleepy head," Chresha said.

He opened his eyes as his vision was a little blurry.

Once his sight became clearer he came to focus on Chresha standing up ass hole naked.

She put her index finger on her lips to ssssh him. Grabbed his hand and led him into the bedroom. She gently closed the door and locked it, got on her knees unbutton, and unzipped his pants grabbed his dick firmly and commenced in attempts to suck the skin off it.

In the process of sucking his dick she could taste and smell pussy; right than and there she knew him and Teressa was fucking while she was at work. she had no problem with it nor was she going to comfront him about it, she figured fuck it let him have his fun.

As he begin squirting his nut down her throat she swallowed it all.....

"Stand up and bend over," Fontane said.....

He pulled his pants to his knees and begin giving her every inch of his dick as she turned her face towards him as is she was looking at him, but in reality she wasn't her eyes was closed. He enjoyed the pleasure of the sight of her ass jiggling, and seeing her fuck faces.

As he begin to nut it felt like the best nut he'd ever released in life, it felt good.

After sexing Chresha went and showered and dressed and woke Teressa up as the three of them went on there expedition of a day, and night filled with excitement.

They kicked it like they were celebrating some sort of victory.....

They started of by simply riding down town area popping bottles as Chresha and Teressa flashed their breast to pedestrians.

They ended up at a dance club.

As they walked in the dance club it was as if they were the center of attraction, as Jay Rule remake of Stevie Wonder's song Giving It Up echoed in the speakers they begin dancing on the dance floor as if they owned it.

They got so drunk at the club that Teressa forget were she was at.

Bottles after bottles, going back and forth to the dance floor, and to the photographer taking pictures all night.

They even found a way to take a few puffs of a little weed in the midst of the of all the cigarette smoke, without security catching them.

That night seemed as if all them became closer to one another.....

On their way home from the club they listened to continious 2Pac CD's in a mildly tone while reminiscing about all the fun times they had over time with, and without each other.

Once they made it to Chresha, and Teressa house Teressa and Fontane went straight to sleep, because the so intoxicated.

Chresha undressed Fontane and Teressa. She took turns sucking on Fontane's dick, and eating Teressa's pussy until she got tired and went to sleep herself.....

After that night Fontane and the girls became real close.

Fontane even stop hanging out with the guys alot because he begin to fall in love with the girls, they had him sprung.

They girls even begin to help Fontane conduct his drug business.

CHAPTER 3

Fontane's connect in Chicago started flooding him with more, and more cocaine; the happiness of love through financial gain came to life, became.

Fontane's connect would supply him with some of the purest cocaine around the town.

Each day Fontane started to make more and more money than he'd normally make.

Fontane didn't sell no petty nickels and dimes he straight weight.

The more money he made the more money the girls were able to enjoy of his.

The twins would go shopping when ever they got ready. The both had numerous cars eqipped with rims, sounds, and Lamborghini doors.

Fontane really loved the girls and would do anything for them.

The twins on the other hand didn't give a fuck about him, they never did.

The only thing they cared about was more dollar signs.

These hoes stop working they had it made.

That was the only reason they started fucking with him in the beginning was to trick him outta all his doe.

They plan was to both begin sexing him, get him to trust them, and trick him into falling in love to benefit off his wealth, and their plan worked.

These hoes had more game Milton Bradley. They was thorough in the way they schemed for money.

Only eighteen but had more game then the average women twice their age.

Their game came from all the things they heard and seen. They had enough game to turn filthy animals clean. They could talk preachers to being sinners, turn losers to winners.

Their mom and dad was drug addicts, the rest of their small family was caught up living their on lives, and really didn't give a fuck about the twins. So at an early age the twins had to scheme for money to survive, and they did it well.

It's a sad repition cycle of broken homes, shattered black family structure contrary to the past times of our lives, of days, lives of yesterday, when blacks lived in two parent homes, only addictions was worshipping God within a sense pleasurable tone.....

Throughout sex they'd take him places he never been before. Not just physically but mentally as well. Those hoes had master the art of seduction.

These hoes was something else.

Although these hoes was only eighteen they looked every bit of twenty five.

They looked like super models. You'd see them and couldn't tell they was ghetto at all.

They was beautiful, lovely and free as artwork of paintings from God to be mutual. Many men would stop and stare imagining if they could have atleast one to love frequently suitable.

The twins stood 5.5 and gorgeous enough to give sight to the blind. Smooth caramel skin with caramel brown eyes to match. They wore no make up because they was naturally beautiful.

The twins were identical, other difference was they wore different hair styles. They always kept their hair down, lips juiced up, and nails, and toes done.

The twins made Fontane feel supreme like a emperor or a king; on top of the world above the clouds as it seems, fairy tale turned to reality formulated from a sweet dream.....

UPCOMING URBAN
NOVEL BY ALAN HINES

KIDNAPPING

CHAPTER 1

It was noon time scorching hot summer's day as the sunlight from the sky lit up the streets, the public was tired of blacks being murdered by the police, and a shame of how black on black crime continuous increase.

It was madness in the city streets two unarmed black males were killed by the punk police; one was home from college pulled over at a traffic stop the police shot and killed him in cold blood, the police lied and said that they thought his cell phone was a gun, the victim had no gun no prior arrest, no criminal background; the other black male that was shot was one of their very own, he was an off duty seargent, the white cops walked up to him to search him assuming he was a street thug, as the off duty seargent went to reach for his badge the racist cops shot him three times in the left side of his chest instantly seperating life from death as the four five bullets ripped through his heart he instantly fell to the concrete visualizing stars as he life no longer existed organs torn apart.

People of all colors came together on and every side of town; north, south, east, and even the west. Through the city streets they marched, and protest only in signs and symbols of peace. Hoping the violence would come to an end, that it would cease.

On Madison street people stood on all four corners as if they owned it. They were together as one, White, Blacks, Mexicans, Puerto Ricans, and even a few Arabics were presents; they all wore t-shirts that displayed Black Lives Matter, some were holding up signs that displayed honk you horn if you love Jesus.

Almost each car that rode past the crowds of people honked their horns; some yelled out there windows, "we love you Jesus," as others yelled out there windows loud and clear, "black lives matter.".....

Daily around the city meetings were being held in churches, unioun halls, amongst various other places but all on one accord to stop the violence.

Hundreds of protestors peacefully marched up to city hall with picket signs, telling those at city hall that the violence just gotta stop.....

The mayor of the city, and the police commisioner came together and made a statement on the news saying that he, and the Chicago police Department will be doing all they can to decrease the violence in the city streets.....

Mysteriously three black teenage girls came up missing, and had been missing for many months; the authorities had no leds to there whereabouts.....

After a innocent twelve year old black girl was killed by stray bullets, her mother was interviewed at the scene of the crime by the channel 9 news......

Running down her face drowning tears of sorrow knowing that her twelve year old daughter was dead wouldn't be here to live to see another day tomorrow. She cried out on the channel 9 news in front of the camera for people stop the violence.

The grieving mother told the news, "the police don't give a fuck about us, if they killing our young black males, what makes everybody think they give a fuck about finding those missing girls. It wouldn't surprise me if they never find the bitch that killed my little girl."

Oh how her angry harsh words was so true.

The authorities searched and searched, did a thorough investigation, but no killer was found and charged with the murder of twelve year old Shante Smith.....

CHAPTER 2

"The niggas off the low-end been eating real good, them niggas been performing," Kuda said. "They been kidnapping niggas, they be trying to grab any nigga getting some real bread," Big Shorty said. "Awwww that's how them niggas been eating like that," Kuda said. "What they do is they kidnapp a nigga for a healthy ransom, or rob a nigga for some weight, and then whatever they get they invest it in buying more weight, flooding the low end with hella narcotics," Big Shorty said. "That's smart," Kuda said.....

Early one sunday morning Kuda sat in the park across the street, slightly up the block from where the shorties slang his rocks.

Big Shorty walked up to Kuda, as Kuda set fire to a Newport long, Kuda took a long pull off the square, as Big Shorty could see, and feel a sense of distress.....

"Man Big Shorty we got to hit us a lick, rob a nigga, kidnap a nigga or something," Kuda said. "Your joint doing pretty good, why you wanna take some other nigga shit," Big Shorty said. "My joint only sell like a stack or two a day, it take me two or three days to scrap up the money to re-copp to go get another four and a baby, you feel me," Kuda said. "But you still eating alot of these niggas out here broke ass hell,"

Big Shorty said, "True, but look at the niggas off the low end they got joints selling 10 or 20 thousand a day, some of them even got two or three joints, selling weight and robbing niggas all at the same damn time, that's what I call getting money," Kuda said.....

Big Shorty remained silent for a brief moment knowing that Kuda was speaking the truth.....

"But Kuda it's so much chaotic madness, that comes along with sticking up. Them niggas off the low-end in constant danger," Big Shorty said. "I'm already in constant danger for all the shootings I've been doing over the years, representing the business for the hood, I deserve to be eating good, fuck the dumb shit I gotta hit me a lick," Kuda said.

Big Shorty remained silent again for a brief moment realizing the realization of what Kuda was talking about.....

Kuda joint started to get sweating more by the police because all ths shooting, that was going on in the area. It was hard for Kuda to work because of the police sweating his joint, and because the hood was in war. Now Kuda really knew he had to hit a lick to get some fast cash.....

More and more Kuda talked to Big shorty about hitting a lick.....

Kuda and Big Shorty ended up getting up with a few guys from the hood that was highly interested in kicking in some doors, and taking another nigga shit.....

A few guys from the hood knew of a few houses on the other side of town where niggas was holding drugs and money at.

Kuda, Big Shorty, and the few guys from the hood kicked in a few doors hitting licks. Each lick they came up on several thousands outta each house, which wasn't shit to them because they had to split it five ways each time. Kuda was hungry to eat, he was tired of small time nickels and dimes he wanted to do it big.....

One of the guys from the hood that they went on the licks with seen how well Kuda, and Big Shorty performed when they ran in them houses, and decided to set them up to kidnapp his sister boyfriend. The guy couldn't do it himself because his sister boyfriend knew him, and he didn't want to send nobody else but Kuda, and Big shorty because other people was messy and would fuck shit up.

The guy sister would be the one to set her boyfriend up, she was tired of the nigga he was to cheap, but the nigga had long money.....

They planned on kodnapping him for thirty thousand, splitting it up evenly four ways a piece, therefore each individual would get seventy-five hundred a piece.....

Kuda was charged up, this is the kind of lick he was interested in hitting.....

Two in the morning as the streets lights lit up the sky, Kuda and Big Shorty set in the car parked several cars behind their soon to be victims car.

Kuda took a long hard pull of the last of his Newport long, inhaling, and exhaling the smoke out of his nose as if it was a blunt filled with loud.

Once Kuda was finish smoking the cigarette he threw the butt out the window.....

Outta nowhere comes this guy sister, and her boyfriend out the door walking down the porch.....

Her and her boyfriend made their way to the back of his car, and started tongue kissing him in which seemed so delghtful for the both of them.

As their lips and tongues disconnected he opened his trunk searching for a purse he had bought her.....

As he lift his head up trying to give her, her bag outta nowhere Kuda appeared instantly back hand slapping the shit out of him upping a big ass gun putting it to his stomach. As Big Shorty came from the back putting a gun to his head forcing him inside the trunk, as the girlfriend cried tears pleading with them to stop; she put on a great performance, she should've won a Oscar for.

As the trunk closed she started smiling, glad that they got his ass. But she continued crying and pleading with them to stop just in a case a neighborhood was watching.

Kuda drove the victim off in his own car as Big shorty followed Kuda in his car; the girlfriend ranned in the house crying as they pulled off.

Once she made it in the house she called her brother and told him, "they got his bitch ass".....

She left out the house went to her car and drove slowly to the nearest police station which took her approximately twenty minutes.....

She ran inside the police station crying emotional tears, that seemed really, real.

She told the police that her boyfriend was kidnapped, she gave up false identities of the kidnappers.

The police asked why didn't she call immediately after it happen. She told the police that the kidnappers robbed her for her phone and money so she couldn't call, and that she went to two of the neighbors house and they never answered their door bells.....

After finishing the police report she went home sipped some wine, relaxed in a hot bubble bath, thinking of the things she'd do with her seventy five hundred once she had it in her possession.....

Two days passed overlapsing into nights; now it was crunch time. Kuda and Big Shorty had made arrangements for the kidnapped victims people to run thirty stacks,

They was supposed to leave the money in a trunk of a car parked near a shopping center that was closed, it was closed because it was the middle of the night, but during the day it would regularly be open.

Before they even made it there with the thirty stacks Kuda, and Big Shorty circled all around the area, there were no police cars or unmarked cars nowhere to be found.

Right before the victims people brought the money, Kuda and Big Shorty watched from a far distance with binoculars as some old lady came, bent down got the keys from under the left back tire as instructed.

As she opened the trunk Kuda, and Big shorty begin cheering, giving each other constant high fives.

She put the money in the trunk and the keys back under the left tire as instructed, and walked away disappearing into the night. Kuda and Big shorty waited for approximately twenty minutes just to make sure the coast was clear, then they text the chick they had designated to go pick the money up.

She made it there in no time. As she walked up to the car bent down picked up the keys from under the left tire, opened up the passenger door.

As soon as she sat down, before she could even close the door, twenty unmarked cars surrounded her out of nowhere, all she heard was sirens and seen guns upped on her from every which way. It was impossible for her to get away.....

The police grabbed her by the neck slamming her face to the concrete, cuffed her up, roughed her up a little and put her in the back of one of the police cars.

The police drove her, and the vehicle that the money was in to the police station to further pursue their investigation.....

Kuda, and Big Shorty watched the whole thing their binoculars, shook the fuck up.....

Once the police left Kuda, and Big shorty pulled off confused not knowing what to do.....

Shortly after leaving the seen of the crime Kuda stopped at a nearby pond and threw his cell phone in it. From Big Shorties phone he called his phone carriers hot line, telling them his phone was stoling and had been missing for hours, he had insurance, so they'd definitely replace it. He threw his phone in the pond, because he text the chick that the police just grabbed from his phone, so if the police went through her phone and linked the text back to his phone he could say it wasn't him, that someone stole his phone.....

As they proceeded back driving home they both was worried, wondering if the girl would play fair ball, or switch up like a bitch and snitch.

Kuda was driving as Big Shorty kept looking back every two or three minutes to see if they was being followed by the cops.

"What the fuck, why is you steady looking back for," Kuda asked? "The police might be following us," Big Shorty said. "The police is not following us if the police wanted us we'd already been got. I hope the bitch didn't tell, I know she did," Kuda said.

"Straight up," Big Shorty said.

Once they made it to the police station at first she played like she didn't speak any English.

She was Boricua, Kuda had nicknamed her the thrill seeking Puerto Rican, because she was adventurous loved violence. Even when the police grabbed her and roughed her up, she loved it.

Months prior to her arrest Kuda, and Big Shorty use to fuck her at the same time; she loved two dicks at once she preferred one in the mouth, and another in her pussy at the same time as Kuda, and Big Shorty would choke her and slap her around in the midst of sex.

She was a bad bitch she just got an adrenaline rush off hardcore shit.....

As the police proceeded questioning her even when they went to get her an interpreter she winded up speaking to them in English.

The cops came to find out her name was Maria Rodriguez. She had been to the joint before twice, once for a kidnapping, and the other time for robbery, and was still on parole for the robbery.

She lied and told the cops that someone paid her to go pick up that car, only because they was pulled over by the police for driving with no license, and once the police left they came back to leave an additonal set of keys under the left tire so she could pick the car up since she had license. To assure them that she had no knowledge of a kidnapping.....

The police knew her story was bullshit, so they asked her who didn't have license and sent her to pick the car up for that reason. She told them she couldn't give any names, because she didn't know what was going on.....

The police pleaded with her for hours to give up a name or names, she didn't tell them shit.

They ended up fingerprinting her processing her in and charging her with kidnapping and sending her to the County Jail. Of course she didn't want to be locked up, but she wasn't worried at all, on her bus ride to the County she'd vision all the pussy she'd be eating once she made it within and started mingling and getting to know the other girls.

After a few days rolled around Kuda, and Big Shorty didn't know what to do with the victim. Normally in a situation like that the individual that had been kidnapped would be put to death since the people got the police involved.

Kuda, and Big Shorty contemplated long and hard about killing the Vic, but decided not to, because if they did they could possibly give Maria a conspiracy to murder, and she could start singing the blues to the police telling them everything.....

After about a week in the middle of the night they dropped the vic off and left him in a abandon building still blindfold and tied up, called his people and the police and told them where to get him from. Kuda and big Shorty wasn't worried about the vic sicking the police on them; he didn't even never see their faces, they had on masks, and even if he did see their faces he didn't know them or there whereabouts because they were from different sides of town.....

After a few weeks Kuda, and Big Shorty was able to get in touch with Maria, she'd call them collect continously.

Come to find out, she was a down bitch, didn't tell the police shit; they kind of figured she didn't snitch because she knew where Kuda, and Big Shorty lived, and if she would've told the police would've been at their house by now.

Kuda and Big Shorty wanted to bond her out, or atleast put up something on her bond, but she couldn't bond out because she was on parole, she had a parole hold.

Kuda and Big Shorty started sending her money orders constantly to make sure she was straight in there.....

The vic they kidnapped continued dating, fucking around with the chick that set him up to get kidnapped, never in his wildest dreams would he even assume that she was the one that set him up to get kidnapped. Later in life he even ended up getting the bitch pregnant with twins.....

CHAPTER 3

B lack lives matter was getting to be an even more major issue. Peaceful protest even seemed to get violent. The black politicians and even black cops was sick and tired of being sick and tired of all the killing blood spilling of the black population.....

More and more teenage black girls would mysteriously come up missing. More and more gangs were waring harder throughout the city, North, South, East, West.....

The black people begin to have meetings quite often mainly at churches, and Union halls.....

One night they had a meeting to their surprise unnumbered white people, and Latinos showed up to support black lives matter; they wore shirts and buttons displaying all lives matter.

The meeting became slightly hostile as not the blacks or Latinos, the white people started snapping out saying that racism does exist, and they were tired of blacks losing their lives by gunfire, especially from white-police officers that gets paid from tax-payers money to serve and protect the community, when all along they were causing the deaths and destruction within the community, it so much killing and hate, seemed as if it was no-love, nor unity.....

They allowed this one white lady to approach the front to get on the stage onto the pulpit, to preach the bullshit.....

"If we study our past history blacks were hung, lynched by white mobs, shot down by angry white fire squads, and even killed by the police as they same way today. With the 1900's many white that committed hate crimes against blacks were either investigated by the police, some even were put on trial and as documenting they were liberated of their crimes. History does repeat itself in a way. Now technology is advance and I've seen with my own eyes on video, shown white police killing black men, and even after shown on video surveillance, the officer still gets acquitted of all charges someway somehow.

If a black man kills another black man he'll immediately be placed in prison until trial, and in large unnumbered cases he'll get found guilty. And if a black man kills a white person in most cases that black man will eventually get found guilty, and sentenced to excessive time in prison possibly until he dies of natural causes. That's one of the main problems with the police brutality and unjustified murders of blacks they know they can get away with it because they are the police. What need to happen is that the police need to start getting persecuted and sent to prison for their crimes of hate. Until they start getting convicted of the crimes the madness won't stop," she said.....

As she dropped the mic tears flowed freely from her eyes. Knowing that racism was still alive. Lucifer's legacy of racism and hate wasn't decreasing any, but instead it begin coinciding with his sick enterprise.

Everyone in the church begin clapping, and cheering impending her speech.....

This one lady sat in the back all the way in the corner dressed in black with a veil over her face as if she was going to a funeral; she cried silently of sorrow drowning watery tears that shall forever shed throughout her lifetime of years wishing it never happen, wishing her son was still living, still here.....A few years prior to that date her son was wrongfully shot down, murdered by the nation, better known as the police; the two officers that killed her son did stand trial, and was acquitted of all charges against them of her sons murder.....

Soon as the second individual stepped to the pulpit to voice his opinion, gun shots rang out, five of em, sounding like a canon was outside.....

Everyone in the church got frightened, and then within rage everyone ran out the church, not scared of the gun-fire, but pissed the fuck off.

They ran out the front door in a rage eagerly trying to see who was standing, and what for.....

As majority of the people had exited the church it was still more rushing out the front door, one woman spotted a guy up the block laid out on the sidewalk.

She yelled out to everyone, "it somebody down there laid out on the sidewalk."

Everybody rushed to the individual that was laid out. Come to find out it was a teenage boy that was still breathing, living. He had been shot once in the ass, and once in both of his legs.....so that meeting was officially over for that night.

As they approached him they seen him shot up as blood ran perfusely down the sidewalk he'd repeatidely keep saying, "I can't believe that pussy ass nigga shot me;

I can't believe that pussy ass nigga shot me; I can't beleive that pussy ass nigga shot me," he said. "Who shot you son," one of the gentlemen in the crowd of church people ask? "I don't know who shot me," he said.

He was lying like a motherfucker, who knew exactly who shot him.

"They called the police already, they should be here soon, it's a police station nearby," the gentlemen said.

In no time flat the police arrived first, and the ambulance arrived shortly after.

The guy that had got shot told the police he didn't know who shot him, although he did. He didn't want the nigga that shot him to get locked up, he wanted to kill the bitch.....

Several days later the guy was let out of the hospital but had to be in a wheel-chair, not for a long-term, only to his ass, and legs were well.....

The same day he was let out of the hospital, the same night the guy that shot him was killed, somebody shot him with a double barrel shotgun taking half his face off.

As homicide started their investigation they called it the face off murder. They never found any witnesses or suspects, so no one was never convicted or even charged with that murder.....

It seemed as if day by day the city streets, begin to be filled with madness, killings, mournings, sirens, and sadness.

It was clicks within the same gangs waring against each other. Rivals was waring against each other even harder. You had certain gangs that was into it with two different gangs at once. Then it was certain gangs that was into it with their own gang and into it with the opps all at the same time.

Part of the reason why gangs was tearing it up with each other was because years prior, and even to the present date the feds was locking up all the heads of gangs; everytime a new head would step up and get in play the Feds would find a way to lock his ass up to, leaving no law and order within the streets amongst; just like a body once you cut the heads of the body will fall. It was uncontrollable anarchy within the city streets.

Throughout the city streets it was constant gun-fire, like it was New Years Eve.

Some of the rappers changed the nickname from The Windy City to The City of No Pity.

Shit got so fucked up they start killing niggas in broad daylight on purpose.....

On one side of town two gangs was waring so hard they just start shooting ata ny and everybody that was affiliated with the oppositions.

One time they caught one of the opps main-girl walking the dog; they shot her and the dog. She lived the dog died.

The same nigga that girl and dog they shot, in return he caught an opp grandma-ma walking home from church with her bible in hand. He walked up to her upped a black .44 automatic to her stomach. Her smile instantly turned into a frown as she said, "praise the lord son," whole heartidely.

As he walked in the alley by gun point she didn't say a word, she wasn't scared at all not one bit, she feared no man but God.

As he walked her to the middle of the alley he seen a car slow down by the alley, he thought it was a detective car; he made her get on her knees on the side of a garbage can, he stood on the side of the garbage can faking like he was pissing. He immediately notice that it wasn't the police.

He looked down at her, she was on her knees praying. She wasn't worried about herself, she was praying for him, praying to the Heavenly Father that he would forgive him for his sins, and that someday he'd convert his life over to the Lord.....

Three shots ripped through her head, leaving her for dead, more blood to shed.

After the third shot many people came out on their back porches, not witnessing the actual murder, but witnessing seeing him fleeing from the scene of the crime.....

What the killer didn't know was that she was more than happy to die or be killed, because she knew that upon death she'd finally meet the king of kings, the lord of lords, God, and his only begotten son Jesus Christ to have eternal peaceful life in Heavens paradise.....

The same day the opps found out who killed his grandmother, him and his guys tore the streets up. The niggas from the other side tore it up as well they went round for round.

It was like a riot in the hoods they were from. They burned down houses, and cars, niggas from each side got shot up bad or killed.

They even burn up some houses waited until the opps came running out and shot them up murdered they ass.....

A few days after grandma was murdered homicide apprehended the killer taking him to jail charging him with that murder. What the killer didn't know was that is that many people witness/saw him running up the alley after he shot her, and that he'd never see the streets again, he'd spend the rest of his natural life rotting away in a jail cell.....

All the violence brought forth more police harrasement of blacks.....

More protesting about Black Lives Matter.

In various places on each side of town you'd see large numbers of people on corners, holding up signs saying honk your horn if you love Jesus, some of the people had on Black Lives Matter T-Shirts, as others had on All Lives Matter T-Shirts. Almost every car that road pass honked their horn, some hollered out "we love you Jesus, Black Lives Matter." A small percentage of passing cars parked their cars joining in on the peaceful protest.....

A few guys in the crowd dipped off to the alley, all you heard was 3 gunshots from a .45 sounded off as the crowds on the streets immediately dispursed. The guys in the alley ran back to the crowds blending in running away as if they didn't know where the shots were coming from, but simply trying to get away from the danger like everyone else. They did that because they joint was right up the street and they couldn't sell their dope with protesters on location, so that quick smart way to get rid of them.

As time progressed along more and more black girls were being kidnapped in various places around the United States; the situation begin to strike controversy, because all of them black.

In the past the black community slightly lost focus on the girls that were being kidnapped, because they found out that a hand full of the missing girls that they thought had been kidnapped, had ran away from home, for different reasons and stayed gone for long periods of time, but eventually returned on their own free will.....

UPCOMING URBAN NOVEL BY ALAN HINES

BLACK KINGS

CHAPTER 1

I t was the middle of the night as the blue, and white police car drove swiftly up the block. The car slowed down as it reached the end of the block as the passenger examined the address of the house to make sure it was the correct address they were looking for.....

Inside the police car was two white police officer's.....

"Is the address 4955," the driver asked the passenger? "Yes it is," the passenger responded.....

The officer's parked their squad car and they bailed out of it swiftly. As they walked up the stairs before they even got a chance to ring the door bell five shots of gun fire rang out....

Two gun shots hit one of officer in the back of the head twice. The other three shots hit the other officer in the back of his head twice, and once in the neck.....

The got shots had came from across the street from the third floor of an abandon building.....

Within seconds Will, and Black was gathering up all their shit trying to swiftly exit the abandon building.....

"Hurry up," Will told Black. "Hold on I drop the banacolus," Black said.....

Once Black picked up the banacolus off the floor, they ran to the stairs, and start running down the stairs at top speed.....

They made it their car which was in front of the abandon building.....

Black made it to the drivers side of the door reached in his pocket, and couldn't find the cars keys, he panicked, and started searching all his pockets.....

"What the fuck unlock the door," Will told Black. "I can't find the keys," Black said, as he continued searching all his pockets, even the back pockets of his pants. "Look in your front pocket, the left one," Will said.

Black stuck his hand all the way in his left pocket and came up with the keys, unlocked the door got in the car reached over and unlocked the passenger side of the car. Started the car up, and got in it, and smashed off with the pedal to the metal, burning rubber.....

At top speed Black was putting forth his best effort to get away.....

"Slow down," Will said. "Slow down, we just killed two police officer's I'm trying to get away," Black said. "Man slow this car down," Will said in a demanding manner.....

Black started to slow down a little.....

"Man slow this car down, you gone get the police to start chasing us. When you do dirt like that you got to leave the scene at ease, that way the police don't get on to you. I'f they see you driving fast that automatically know what it is. Now if they see you driving regular with your seat belt on blending in with the hundreds of cars passing by they are less likely to try to get at you. Even if you drive right pass them after doing dirt, as long as you're driving regular nine times out of ten they aint gonna fuck with you, becuase they'll think you a regular car just driving past," Will said.....

Black slowed the car down driving at regular speed.....

They drove to a secret hide away only to stash the guns. Then they drove to another secret hide away where the usually have meetings.....

Once they made it there Will begin to think about what they just had did, and the mistakes they made.....

"You did a good job, but the way we did that was messy, we got to make it better next time. We can't slip up and drop things like we did the banacolus, and we definitely can't misplace car keys. You keep it in your mind exactly where the car keys are at. Just think if we wouldn't have found those keys we'd probably had to make it home on foot, chances are we would've been chased by the police or even caught. We would've looked real suspicious walking down

136

the street dressed in all black carrying large equipment concealed in bags," Will said.....

"You know that no matter what happens whenever you do dirt like that you must not tell nobody not even those that's part of the Black National family," Will said.

Black remained quiet staying attentive listening to Will as Will would feed his brain powerful knowledge.....

Will, and Black were part of an organization called Black Nationals. Will was the founder of Black National, Black was the co-founder. Some may would've considered them a gang, but the Black Nationals considered themselves to be an organizations that was in existence for the upliftment of black people.

The Black Nationals was a small organiztion that consist approximately thirty members. Every once in a while they'd accept a new member. Only in meetings they'd wear all black. They did a little protesting, and preaching in schools, and churches. But mainly they focus on trying to get blacks education, on a higher level of higher learning so that blacks would be successful on a positive note. When they did their protesting, and preaching they didn't represent Black National, they represented for the black people. Black National was like a secret society.

The Black Nation was against crime, and any usage of drugs, alcohol, and tobacco usage. The only crimes that the Black nationals was up with was violent hate crimes against white people.....

The next day after they killed them two police Black Nationals held a meeting in one of the members basement that was made up like a church. Will led the meeting as usual.....

"It's about the growth, and developement of the black community. We are black, and beautiful, black beauty's. It's time for change, and improvement, and we must do what it takes to change, and improve. We were once kings, and queens we ruled the place we once lived in before the white devils came in. We governed, and control our own lands. Our women even walked around bare chested showing of their beautiful black breast not as a sex symbol to men, but as a way of being. The women did this until the white devil came along, and made it seem wrong. As we go back the Alpha in bible the snake Satan tricked Adam, and Eve into thinking nudity was an impurity, and abnormal the white devils did the same to us. Every black brother, and sister in the divine area right now hug one another, as a form of undying love unity for your black brothers, and sisters" Will said to the Black Nationals as they all stood at attention dressed in all black unlocking their hands from behind their backs to tightly hug one another listening vividly to Will as he continued to preach.....

Overtime the Black National's membership slightly grew, as the Black Nationals terror of vicious hate crimes dramatically increased.....

One late cold winter's night Ruby ran up to an parked squad car occupied by two white officer's with her coat open, and her shirt slighty torn with her big beautiful brown breast bouncing.....

"He tried to rape me, he tried to rape me," Ruby said to the officers.....

The officer was so mesmerized by the sight of those big ole titties, that they wasn't able to respond right back it was as they were in a trance.....

Within no time the officer's came back to reality.....

Both officer's got out of the car.....

"Who tried to rape you," one officer asked with his eyes on her breast. "Where he at," the other officer asked with his eyes stuck on her breast. "He in this alley," Ruby said.....

Ruby ran back to the alley as the police got in the squad car to follow her.

As they made it to the part of the alley were Ruby was at they wondered why she didn't get in the car with them instead of running back to the alley on her own.

They rushed out of their car before they could say a word Ruby sprayed them in the face with Mace. Then she begin cutting one in the face back to back, as he grabbed his gun busting shots unable to see due to the Mace in his eye he accidently shot his partner in the eye twice. The bullets went to his brain instantly leaving him for dead.

The Mace in the officer's eyes made him feel as if he was blind, as Ruby stabbed in his throat a few times he dropped his gun, as he himself collapsed to the ground Ruby got on top of him stabbing in both his eyes, his face, and his head, as he squealed like a pig, Ruby snatched his life away from him.....

After the short period of drama Ruby vanished away from the scene of the crime.....

Ruby was a member of the Black Nationals, she was thoroughbred, had more heart then most of the members in the Black Nationals, and she knew how to do her dirt smart, and kept her mouth shut.....

Days later Ruby walked up to some of the Black National members as they were discussing the two police getting killed. Never in their wildest dreams would they have imagined that Ruby was the one who killed the two police.....

Didn't nobody know what Ruby did, she had learned from Will to do dirt, and to keep your mouth close, that way you wouldn't have to worry about no one telling the police.....

Sometimes members of the Black Nationals would do dirt to white people by themselves, and keep their dirt to themselves; other times they'd get together in numbers to do dirt, they called it war games.....

One late quiet night Will, Black, Ruby, and two other members of Black National, Dennis, and Tody, all decided to play war games. Sometimes they'd split up to play war games. This time they decided to do it together, but in two different cars that would be right behind one another.

They'd use the women as driver's so that way after they did their dirt the men could duck down in the cars as if the women were in the car driving by themselves; that way it would be less likely the police to bother a car only occupied by one woman. Will, Black, and Ruby was in one car. Tody, and Dennis trailed behind them in their car.....

While driving on a quiet side street unexpectedly they spotted a black prostitute just finished performing hardcore erotica for a white trick in a white Sedan. Black whom was sitting in the back seat of the first car signaled Todie, and Dennis to pull over.

Both cars pulled over on the other side of the street a short distance from the white trick in the sedan, and cut their lights off swiftly. The prostitute exited the car, and walked swiftly anxious to spend her earned money on buying her some dope.

He was so mesmerized by the sexual experience he just had with the prostitute that he sat in the car smoking a cancer stick oblivious to his surroundings and what was soon to come.....

Outta nowhere three shots sounded off like canons, "dooock, dooock, dooock." One bullet hit the white trick in the bottom part of the back of his head the other two hit him in his back.

Will felt wonderful after he shot the man up three times, as he ran back to the car the sounds of victorious trumpets sounded off in his head.....

As Will made it to the car all three men in both cars duck down, as the ladies smoothly coasted off as if nothing never happen the way Will taught them how to do it.....

"Did you get him, did you kill him," Ruby asked excitedly? Will begin slightly laughing. "I don't know I hope so," Will said.

About an hour later they found another victim. A white guy dressed up in a three piece suit walking down the street as if he owned the street with a briefcase in his hand.....

They pulled both cars around the corner Will got out and walked up to the man. As Will approached him the white gentleman looked up at Will with a smile upon his face on verge of greeting him. Will upped on him hitting him three times in the forehead the bullets ripped through his skull pushing half of his head off. The sight off it made Will so happy.

Will ran back to the cars jumping for joy.....

What Will didn't know was that the man he had killed was a homicide detective whom was coming home from work. The detective decided to walk home from work instead of driving, because his head was clouded by the constant murders, and secretive racism that was going on in his precinct, and around the world in general. The detective was on his way home to be with his black wife, and his two bi-racial kids.....

Later that night both car loads were mad, and jealous that Will had did all the killings himself that night. It was almost daybreak, and they had decided to call it a night. Ruby spotted this older white guy standing a bus stop on a main street.

She pleaded with Will to let her kill him. Will told her no the women were only used in war games to assist the men to get away. Ruby debated with Will that men, and women should be as equals especially the black men, and women. Although Ruby, and Will only debated for a short period of time Will decided to let her free to commit murder.

Both cars pulled around the corner, and parked, Will reloaded the gun handt Ruby the gun, and told her to be careful. Once Ruby got out of the car Tody, and Dennis looked at her stun with no clue of what was going on.

As Ruby started to walk to her destination Will got out the car, and told Tody, and Dennis that Ruby was getting to kill the white chump at the bus stop.....

As soon as Will got back in his car, and slammed the door he heard six shots go off. The shots was so loud that it was if the were coming from only a few feet from him.....

Ruby had walked up to the white guy on the bus stop, and asked for a cigarette the white guy made a racial slur, as Ruby upped on him shot him up six times unloading her .38 revolver as the bullets ripped through his flesh she knew he wouldn't live through tips of hallows to see a better day tomorrow.....

In no time Ruby made her way back to the car got in the driver's side, and smoothly coasted off.....

As they drove away to their secret hide away they all visioned Ruby taking away that white chumps life.....

Right then, and there Will knew Ruby was a winner, and a proud member of Black National's.....

Overtime Will wondered, and wondered how would it be possible for his dream of Black Nationlism to come to reality. He wondered how would blacks begin to govern politics in their own communities, how would blacks become more book smart through education, and how would their be more blacks becoming business owners.....

Will, Black, amongst others in the Black National worked for the white men. And those that didn't work for the white men were either mechanics or beauticians whom didn't have their own shops yet. But all of the Black Nationals had one thing in common they all long for the day to come were they all lived like kings, and queens on earth legitimately without any crimimal grinding.....

"Black beauty's I'd like to thank each, and every one of you for showing up today it's my privilege to be part of this organization.

Since we first started it's been all talk, and not enough action. We gotta figure out a way for improvement," Will said as everyone started to clapping, and cheering.....

Everyone started clapping and cheering because they'd been feeling the same way.....

Within the next meeting Will had came up with a plan to make black people slightly advance. He told them that were mechanics, and beautician to train other blacks those trades; not just the blacks in Black National, but black people in general. Will told them to do that so that they would be able to make extra money outside of their day jobs, and eventually be able to take their trade and earn money, and be able to open up small shops. Will also told the Black Nationals to go to libraries, and attend college to study politics, that way they'd be able to slightly advance on a political level. The Black Nationals followed instructions.....

Within only weeks Will would talk to members of Black National, and he could tell by their conversations that they'd followed orders. Will felt good that he planted mental seeds of growth that was slowly starting to grow.....

Over time the Black Nationals continued to play war games. The war games had slowed down dramatically, most of Black National was more interested in the knowledge of being book smart.....

Ruby, and Will feel in love with war games, most of the time when they played them it would be just them two.....

One night after playing war games Will, and Ruby decided to go over his house to spend a night simply because it was late, and both of them were to sleepy to drive far. Will lived closer to where they was at than Ruby did so that's why they decided to go to his house. It was cool because Ruby's husband was a part of Black National, and Will girlfriend whom didn't live with him was real cool with Ruby, and her husband.....

Once they almost made it to Will's house it started to rain. When they made to Will's place they couldn't find a park therefore they had to park all the way up the street, and get out and run to his house in the rain in which left they clothes all wet up.....

"You can go in my bedroom, and look in the closet my girlfriend left some clothes of hers in there, you can get a pair of her clothes, get in the shower, and change clothes. You can sleep in my bedroom I'll just sleep on the couch," Will said.....

Will sat the couch feeling uncomfortable because of the wet clothes, and because he was fighting his sleep he wanted to wait until Ruby was done so he could get in the shower.....

Within a few minutes Ruby came out the bathroom ass hole naked with only a towel drying off her hair. Will stood to attention looking at Ruby as if he'd just seen a ghost.....

"Ruby what are you doing," Will asked? "I'm drying my hair," she said calmly, and innocently. "Ruby where your clothes at," Will asked? "They're in the bathroom. I remembered what you had said at a meeting one time that we were free to walk around naked in Africa before the white man came, and poisioned our minds," Ruby said.

Their stood this naked beautiful black young lady. She stood five feet, chocolate super thick with such a cute face, and naturally curly hair.....

This girl on some bullshit, she know she married to one of our black brothers, and she want to put me in this situation, Will thought to himself.....

She stopped drying her hair off dropped the towel on the floor and walked up to Will, and gently hugged him around his waist, as he didn't attempt to reject. She looked him in his eyes and told him, "I love you." "But you're married," he said. "But I'm only human, and I love you, and I want you take me as your queen, and do whatever you want to me, I belong to you," she said. Will begin smiling, and laughing right before their lips connected, as they began playing the French kissing game that seemed like forever.....

Eventually Ruby snatched her lips away from his and fell to her knees. She looked up at him, and asked him, "can I suck your dick." "Go ahead," he said.

Ruby eagerly broke the button off his pants, and then unzipped them. Once she pulled his dick out of his underwear she paused speechless she couldn't believe how long, and fat his dick was, she had never seen or had a dick that big.....

She wrapped her left hand around the back of the dick, then she tried putting it in her mouth she almost couldn't open her mouth wide enough to put it in but she finally did.

She stroked the back of his dick with her left hand as she ate his dick up as if she was hungry craving for it. She was sucking it vigoursly as if she was trying to suck the skin off of it, and shove it down her throat, and stroking it with her hand, all at the same damn time.

I love Ruby, I hope she never stop sucking my dick, Will thought to himself. At that instant moment she stopped took her mouth off his dick, and spit on his dick five times. Will couldn't believe she had just spit on him. She immediately started back sucking his dick. Will immediately felt how better it was after the moisture of the spit. Within seconds she paused and spit on his dick three more times back to back. Once she started back sucking on it the spit ran down her face which made her look like a sick dog foaming at the mouth.....

In no time flat Will was unleashing nut in her mouth as she drunk, and swallowed all of it like a champ.....

Afterwars Ruby laid on the couch on her back with her eyes shut thinking to herself like this guy getting ready to kill this pussy with that big ass dick, and he did just that.....

Will had her hollering, and screaming half the night. Before the night was done he even bust her the ass.....

After that night they promise not to let their sex interfere with their personal lives.....

CHAPTER 2

B lack entered Will's home.....

"Guess what happened," Black said. "What happened," Will asked? "I've been drafted to go fight in nam," Black said. Will paused, he couldn't believe what his ears were hearing.....

"That's sad," Will said in low tone of voice.

"Everything we've been through, all the efforts we put forth to be black powerful superior to the devils, and they pulled this stunt. They don't want to treat us as equals but now they want you to fight their war," Will said. "I aint going Imma skip town," Black said. "You can't skip town, that's a case, you gone to have to do a prison term when they catch up with you, that's a federal case I think they call it draft dodging or something like that," Will said. "So what would you do if they drafted you for war," Black asked? "I don't know, that's a good question. I might just go and kill up some of them Orientals. I think I'd rather try my luck on the battle field, than spend a long term in prison," Will said.....

Will, and Black paused for a moment in time as their minds was flooded with alot of unanswered questions, as they visualized the battle fields in Vietnam, death and destruction, and the past history of the white men hate, instead of loving.....

Within the upcoming days Black decided to go to fight the war in Vietnam.....

"Good evening my black, and beautiful people," Will said to the Black National Organization. "Good evening," the Black National Organization said back to Will simultaneously.....

"We were all design, and taught to be warriors to live, eat, and breed, on a militant mind settings, we have military minds.

That comes from ancient African tribes that's the way we survived and ruled our lands as soilders of war. Right now the white man has his own personal war going on, and forces us to fight it, due to their laws we have no other choice if called upon. No matter what happens don't let the white people tear you down mentally nor physically. Stick your chest out, and hold your head up, and concur all obstacles.....To the devils we are ugly to me we're all black, and beautiful," Will said full-heartedly.....After that meeting the Black Nationals begin to think more about the art of war.....

A couple weeks later Black was shipped of to Vietnam nervous, and worried about if he'll make it through alive. At this time Black was only twenty one years old, Will was only twenty years old, Ruby was twenty three. Majority of the Black Nationals were young, but they had the brains of people twice their age.....

Will decided to quit his job working for the white man. He felt as if he should practice what he preach. Will knew how to cut hair so he started cutting hair, as a hustle, and it paid of instantly.....

Once Black first made it to the U.S. soilders overseas he noticed that the soilders had to do extreme workouts. And he knew that his turn on the battle field was soon to come.....

After a period of training Black was sent to the battle field for war. He was nervous like never before in life, but he didn't let it show.

During his first few times on the battle fields he was lucky they didn't come across any enemy troops.....

His first time coming across enemy troops was one late night as the mosquitos constantly ate away at the soilders flesh as the hot dreary night seemed endlessly they walked across dry land as Black, as well as the other soilders hoped that they didn't step on a land mind which would be a painful death they made it to a small body of water which was only approximately two feet high.

They crossed the water, and made it to these short bushes. As they stood still in the water in which seperated them from dry land they looked in them, and seen a small camp of enemy troops.

The general gave signal with his hand for everyone to remain silent. Then the general used his fingers as a sign language giving orders in the way to attack.....

146

Black became even more nervous each second. He knew it was time for war, time to seperate the boys from the men.....

In no time the soilders were attacking enemy troops the sounds of on going rapid gun fire that flooded the sound waves of ears as grenades sounded off like rocket launchers. You could hear crying, screaming, yelling in different languages as death, and destructions became one.....

Once that battle was over the U.S stood triumphant, their was casulties of war on both sides. Majority of the casulties was that of the enemy troops. Those that the U.S. didn't put to death fled the camp.....

That night Black seen how prosperous the art of surprise could be......

Overtime Black experienced more episodes of being front line on the battle field, as soilders were constantly getting killed, Black started to like war fair.....

Overtime the other soilders begin to call Black, God. They nicknamed him God because everytime they'd go onto the battle field it seemed as if he had God on his side.....

Will, and Black stayed in constant contact mainly through letters, occasionally over the phone they'd talk.....

Black would tell Will how intense the war in nam was, and that it made their war games seem like a joke. Will told Black that the Black National were starting to rotate with the ViceLords. Black didn't like it, Black knew the ViceLords was a street gang.....

Will had met some of the outstanding members of ViceLords by cutting hair. Will had came to find out that they had some of the same exact concepts that Black Nationals had. They were even getting funded from the goverment to help uplift the black community, as a sign of thanks and reparation for blacks helping building this country which was long overdue.....

Will had been introduced to the minister of ViceLords. The minister instantly took a liking for Will because he was smart, and he showed the qualities of a leader.....

Overtime Will had did alotta dirt for the minister, Will would bring nightmares of death, and blood shed to reality for the minister.....

Within time Will, and majority of the Black Nationals became ViceLords, the minister made Will a five star universal elite.....

The king of ViceLord kept hearing good things about Will and decided to start rotating with him a little. The king didn't rotate with to many people heavy; He loved people, but didn't trust no one.....

The king of ViceLord rotated with Will a little turned into alot. The king had never met someone so young, so thorough, and so dedicated to the upliftment of ViceLord, and the upliftment of the black community.....

At this point in time the ViceLords wasn't very deep but they we're on fast uprise. They mainly resided on the west side of Chicago. Their were a few in the surrounding suburbs, but they wasn't that deep.....

Will would go out, and do recruiting, and go out and provide knowledge, and finance, and whatever assistance he could to the black community.....

In no time flat Will was a supreme elite, and had jurisdiction to create gang literature that the ViceLords had to abide by. He also had the kings blessings to start his own branch of ViceLord if he decided he wanted to do that.....

Will worked on the literarure of ViceLord with the king, and the minister, and now had expectations in becomming the king of his own branch of Vicelord.....

Within the matter of months Will finally decided to start his own branch of ViceLord, his branch would be the Traveler ViceLords, T.V.L.....

Mainly but not all branches of ViceLord name derived from ancient African tribes.

The Traveler tribe was an ancient tribe from Africa that traveled to conquer other tribes but not in war, but using their brains to manipulate them to became as one. The traveler tribe would find out were slave ship were and go to kill white slave traders, sometimes they'd became successful, other times they'd come up unsuccessful slaughtered like animals, but those that would survive would continue on, on their missions.....

Their were many other ancient African tribes; the Mandego's, the Zulu's, the Shabazz, the Ghosts, but Will decided to use the Travelers name because they were more in the likeness of himself, and his beliefs.....

Will became the youngest king of any branch of ViceLord that ever existed.....

CHAPTER 3

A fter a year, and a half fighting in Vietnam Black's tour of duty was over, he was sent back home. He couldn't wait to touch the city streets again.....

Will went to pick up Black from the airport in one of his new cars. As they drove, and reminisced Will took Black through the areas were ViceLords dwelled Black was impressed.

Will took Black through the areas were they Travelers was, and Black couldn't believe how Will had blossomed in the streets while he was gone.

Black was impressed by Will's street growth, but still had the Black National concept embedded in his mind frame in which he didn't believe in Will's committing crimes.....

As the day turned to night Will took Black through one of his spots were they sold his dope at.

The spot was inside a small building, the dope fiends would go into the front door, and walk shortly to a door with a slot in it where the mail man would stick their mail in. The dope fiends would slide their money through that slot, and tell the people on the other side of the door exactly how many bags of dope they were interested in purchasing.

Will had someone in the front of the building on security so when the police come they could get rid of all the drugs, the money, and the gun. They'd get rid of it by quickly taking the front part of their vent off, and giving it to the neighbors, or they would just give it to one of the neighbors up stairs; the upstairs neighbors would drop a long cord down for them to load up their merchandise in when, and if the police ever came....

Will, and Black sat across the street on top of the hood of Will's car checking out the business. Black couldn't believe how many customers were constantly coming, and how much money Will had to be making off all them customers.....

Many of the Black Nationals became Travelers. Those they didn't become Travelers still did things to uplift the black people in their on way, and time.

The Black Nationals never told anyone, about their involvement with Black National, or the war games they played. They all kept it secret, they didn't even tell the Travelers that wasn't initially Black Nationals, about Black Nationals.

From time to time the ex-Black Nationals continued to play war games.....

After they left Will dope spot they went to see all of the ex-Black Nationals. All of them was more than happy to see Black home from the war.....

The last ex-Black National member they went to see was Ruby. Tears of joy ran down Ruby's face; she was so happy that he made it home safe, because so many people was getting killed in that war.....

Will ended up dropping Black off at his moms house, and went to meet Ruby at his own house.....

Will went, and jumped in the shower, as Ruby sat on the couch with the tip of her finger in her mouth, sucking on it as if she was a shy teenage girl.

Will came out of the bathroom wearing a robe.

As Will robe dropped to the ground Ruby took off her dress in which she had no panties, no bra. She dropped to her knees, with purple lipstick on she gently placed Will's dick in her mouth begin humming and bobbing back, and forth doing her best to make him fill pleasure, and love through the art of dick sucking.....

Ruby, and Will had got real close, but they kept their loving a secret. Ruby loved Will as if was he an angel on earth. Will loved Ruby, adored her sex, but loved his real girlfriend even more.....

The next morning Will went to go pick up Black. Will took Black shopping for clothes, and took him to the car lot, and brought him a brand new Cadillac.....

As Black started driving the area in his new lac with Will in the passenger seat a dude named Smurf spotted them, and flagged them down. As they parked Smurf ran to the passenger seat, and Black easily raised down the window.....

"William, Dirt robbed me," Smurf said. "Don't never call me William, call me Will. My Dirt, Traveler Dirt robbed you," Will said. "Yep, he robbed me last night, I was looking for you all night, you was no where to be found. I was gone took care of my business, but I can't bring no hurt, harm, or danger to one of the ViceLord brothers, that's just like doing something to one of my family members," Smurf said. "How much he rob you for," Will asked? "A bill, and a quarter," Smurf said. "One, twenty-five," Will said, and then reached in his pocket pulled out a roll of money, counted out a hundred, and twenty five dollars, and gave it to Smurf.

"That's good the way you went about the situation. By us being black men, and ViceLords all of us are like family, well atleast we suppose to be like family. But T.V.L. is like my immediate family. Like I just said it's good that you went about it the way you did, 'cause if you ever cross me, and do something to anybody claiming T.V.L. it's gonna be killer clowns, guns that explode, and burning of eternal fire all at once as a rapture you must feel," Will said. "Come on William, I meant to say Will you know I wouldn't never do nothing to none of the Travelers," Smurf said. "I heard that slick shit you said out your mouth, talking about you was gonna handle your business. As long as I'm living, and breathing you or nobody else aint gone do shit to no Traveler, and if you do you aint gone get away with, so don't let me hear nothing like that come out your mouth again. Just meet me in the pool hall tomorrow around twelve thirty, or one, we gone enforce law on dirt," Will said. "Alright, I'll be there," Smurf said as he stepped away from the car, as Black pulled off.....

"I been knowing you for umteen years, and you make everybody call you Will. Whats wrong with calling you William, thats your full name," Black said. "Yes, you have known me for umteen years, and you been calling me Will for umteen years so just stick with it," Will said. "Well from now on call me God," Black said. "I'm not calling no other man God," Will said. "That's my name, they gave me that name while I was at war. They gave me that name because each time I'd go to battle I'd always stand triumphant, and I'd always make it back safe," Black said. "Okay then God," Will said possessing a big smile on his face.....

The next morning Will, God, and some of the ViceLords were in the pool hall shooting pool. Some where smoking cigars, while others were sipping cheap wine, while others were doing both. Will, didn't smoke or drink.....

While shooting pool Will kept looking out of the window to across the street. Will had a dime bag powder spot across the street. He kept looking over there observing the customers in, and out the indoor spot.....

Will winding up sending someone to get Dirt.....

About an hour later in comes Dirt through the pool hall door with one of the other Lords by his left side.....

"Will you was looking for me," Dirt said, as everyone in the pool hall stopped what they was doing, and got quiet. Before Will answered Dirt, Dirt noticed Smurf standing over in the cut. Dirt immediately put his hand on his gun which was tucked in the waist of his pants. Then he gave Smurf a mean mugg, a cold stare, that of a villing from a nightmare.

Reality immediately came forth Dirt now knew what Will had wanted him for.

Although Dirt wasn't at all worried about Smurf pulling a stunt in the presence of Will he still clutched his gun just to let Smurf know if he got out of his body he'd be feeling the pain of bullets.....

Dirt step closer to Will as everyone including Smurf surrounded him.....

"This brother said you robbed him," Will said to Dirt. "Yeah I robbed him so what he aint no Traveler, he a Renegade, fuck 'em," Dirt said.....

All the other ViceLords that wasn't Travelers, and those that was frowned up in disgust.

"So what he aint no Traveler, he still a ViceLord. That's why I be telling ya'll to learn ya'll lit, then ya'll will know how to conduct ya'll self as ViceLords. Now if this brother would've came back and did something to you the Travelers would've had to murder the Renegades making them extinct going against the laws, and policies of ViceLords, and killing of our own black brothers," Will said as everyone remained speechless.....

"You gotta learn your lit, you in violation for baring arms against a member of ViceLord, disobeying the laws of ViceLord unity, and jeopardizing the body of ViceLord. Normally you suppose to get a minute for each charge, but by this being you first time in violation you gone get one minute from head to toe. Big C collect all the weapons from all the brothers in this room," Will said.

Big C was a Conservative ViceLord..... Always at meetings, or when a brother was in violation there was to be no weapons, because meetings, and violations were considered to be somewhat spiritual, sacret, and uplifting.....

Once Big C collected all the weapons from the brothers they all tucked in their shirts faced the east, bowed their heads closing their eyes, lifting their palms up.....

God stood in the cut watching everything amazed about how the ViceLords orchestrated things.....

Big C started to read the Statement of Love, "For you my brother my love begins at birth that has manifested itself throughout our heritage for the color of our skin which is black. For I am you, you are me. Our minds are for the same cause. Our efforts are for the same goals. Our souls bound for the same destination. Our lives are for the same new nation. For you my black brother I give my unity, my vitality, my undying love, almighty."

Once Big C was done reading the statement they all opened their eyes, and lifted their heads up.

Dirt stood against the wall.

Will looked at his watch then in a matter of seconds he gave Big C the go ahead, to violate Dirt.

Big C hit dirt in the face once, Dirt fell to the floor as Big C continued violating him for a minute.

After the violation Dirt stood to his feet body aching in slight pain, he shook each ViceLord hand, and then hugged them.

He shook hands, and hugged Will last. As he hugged Will, Will whispered in his ear, "learn your lit."

Afterwards Dirt, and the guy he came in the pool hall with left, and everybody started back playing pool, smoking, drinking, and laughing as if nothing never happen.....

God started to fall in love with the way the ViceLords did things.....

Will and God left the pool hall.....

"That was raw the way you did things back there, what was that, that guy was reading," God asked? "That was the Statement of Love, that's a piece of ViceLord literature, I'm the one that wrote it. Alot of ViceLord literature I wrote. I took alot of Black Nationals concept, and turned them into ViceLord concepts, and wrote it up in literature. Me or none of the others that was once Black National told the ViceLords about the Black National, I'll take that secret to the grave with me," Will said. "Literature I didn't even know gangs had literature," God said. "We not actually a gang we're a nation of people that's about the upliftment of black people. ViceLord is design to uplift the black people," Will said.....

God stopped at a stop sign and pulled out a cigarette, and set fire to it, and begin puffing.....

"You smoke cigarettes, you digging yourself an early grave. Black Nationals, are not to use drugs, alcohol, or smoke tobacco," Will said. "Black Nationals, don't suppose to commit crimes, unless they were hate crimes," God said, and then inhaled, and exhaled cigarette smoke. "But I commit crimes, for the uplifting of the community. I sell alotta drugs, but I take the money, and invest it into good things within the black community," Will said. "You tearing down the black community, selling them drugs," God said. "But if I don't sell it to them it's many others that will. But I promise you majority of my money is being invested into positive things that will make blacks prosperous in the future," Will said.....

Within the upcoming weeks God noticed that Will was serious, because he seen with his own eyes how Will helped blacks with the money he made off drugs. Will would give black churches large sums of money, provided blacks with places to live outside of the ghetto, help people with their bills, and donate money to schools for better, advanced books, so blacks could get a higher learning.....

God start to see with his own eyes how the goverment would help fund ViceLord; and that the ViceLord would do many things for the black community, such as help blacks find jobs, provide after school programs so that the kids could come there to study, and have fun, amongst other things.....

God started to spend time with ex-Black Nationals that had become Travelers he noticed that none of them were in the streets selling drugs, or committing crimes they were working in places of after school programs, drug treatment centers in the black community or in college working on degrees.....

In no time God became a Traveler. He went from having no status to a branch elite, that dictated only to Traveler ViceLords, to a universal elite that dictated to all Vicelords, then to the prince of T.V.L. And he earned his way up to that title......

The Traveler ViceLords, amongst other branches of ViceLords rapidly grew, and spreaded throughout the city, and to the surrounding suburbs.....

Will, and God both became amazed with numbers of membership growth. Many all through the westside of Chicago wherever you went you seen guys with their hats broke to the left flagging ViceLord.

God started to apply his military experience in Vietnam to the ViceLord structure. In the military when soilders were punished for minor things they'd only have to do a harsh workout. God put within ViceLord law that if a representitive of ViceLord did something minor to break law they wouldn't have to get violated physically, but they would only have to do a harsh work out. The king of all ViceLords, and the minister liked that concept.

The minister of ViceLord put Will and God in play to be his personal assistances with creating more diplomatic ViceLord literature.....

God wrote his first piece of Vicelord lterature called ViceLord Life:

ViceLord Life
In the scriptures of life let it be of the creators will and might to project and show liberty and disadvantages of life.
But let life be a test and delight.
Always honor, guard, and protect brothers and sisters of ViceLord life.
Let it be done here and on a positive note uplifting to show growth to others in life.
Be forever real, be forever ViceLord with-through, upon a ViceLords life.

God's second piece of literature he wrote was called Concepts of Men:

Concepts of Men

Policies, concepts, and the conduct of men.
Honoring the five points of the golden star to withstand.
Love, truth, peace, freedom, and justice to the blackmen.
Utilizing knowledge and intellect to advance.
Remain sane dealing with circumstances.
Uplifting the brothers as much as you can.
Obey the unity, policies, concepts, codes, and
conduct of being a black man.

After God wrote those first two pieces of lit, and put them in ViceLord literature the king of ViceLord, and the minister depending on God for more knowledgeable lit to add within ViceLord literature.....

The king of ViceLords, and the minister was honored to have Will, and God as outstanding members Of ViceLord; the king, and minister was amazed on how young, intelligent, and dedicated to uplifting the black community Will, and God was. What the king, and minister didn't know that Will, and God thrived off Black Nationalism long before they became Vicelords. What Will, and God didn't know was that the king, and minister was grooming them to be the king, and prince of not only the Travelers, but of all ViceLords.....

URBAN NOVEL ALREADY PUBLISHED BY ALAN HINES.

BOOK WRITER

CHAPTER 1

Suzie and Carl sat at the table using dope.

"How many more bags of dope we got left," Carl asked Suzie while scratching and nodding all at the same time. "We got five mo bags of dope, why you didn't bring no rocks back so I can smoke me some primos," Suzie asked? "I couldn't the joint got hot the nigga who was working the rock packs disappeared, the only reason I brought some dope home is because every time I sold a blow jab, I kept me a couple blows for myself instead of selling them, I'm glad I did cuz the nigga who was working the blow jab disappeared to when the police came through. I know they wondering where the fuck I'm at I was supposed to work for the rest of the day, I'm just gone tell them I left cuz some police came through that had locked me up before," Carl said.

Carl continued scratching and nodding as if he was sleep for a few seconds. He slightly opened his eyes and looked up at Suzie . . . .

"This dope a bomb, this dope better than the dope they had yesterday," Carl said. "Yeah I know I think they put some new shit on the dope, whatever they putting on it they need to keep putting it on it," Suzie said.

Carl upped his dick . . . .

"Bitch suck this dick," Carl said. "I told you about calling me out my name, put your dick up before Latisha come in," Suzie said. "Aw yeah I forget she was in there, I'm glad she didn't walk in here while I had my dick out," Carl said . . . .

Ten seconds later in comes Latisha . . . .

"Mom I'm hungry give me some money so I can get me something to eat," Latisha said. "Girl I brought you something to eat yesterday," Suzie said. "But that was yesterday, what I only supposed to eat once a week," Latisha said. "Girl don't be getting smart at the mouth. I wish I would've listen to my momma and got an abortion when I was pregnant with you," Suzie said.

"Here girl here go ten dollars, and bring me some candy back," Suzie said.

Every time this bitch get high she always want to suck on some candy, Latisha thought to herself.

On her way to the store she ran into one of her little friends Jennifer . . . .

"Where are you going Latisha," Jennifer asked? "I'm on my way to the store to get my dope fiend ass momma some candy," Latisha said. "Why do dope fiends always gotta have candy when they get high off dope," Jennifer asked? "I don't know, I be wondering the same thing," Latisha said.

"My birthday is tomorrow," Jennifer said. "My birthday is in a couple of weeks," Latisha said. "Fo real," Jennifer said. "Fo real, I'll be eleven," Latisha said. "I'll be twelve," Jennifer said.

"Let me go get my momma this candy, cuz this bitch gone be tripping if it take me to long to come back with her candy," Latisha said. "Stop by here when you come back," Jennifer said. "A'ight," Latisha said . . . .

As Latisha made it within the store she noticed that all three lines were long as hell.

She went into the section where the candy was . . . .

What should I get candy bars, or jolly ranchers, fuck it I'll get one of each, Latisha thought to herself.

She went to get in a long ass line to pay for the candy . . . .

While waiting in line she begin to think about what was she going to order from the restaurant next door . . . .

I'mma order me a cheese burger, fries, and a slurpy, she thought to herself . . . .

The line continued to move slow . . . .

I'm tired of waiting in this line, Latisha thought to herself . . . .

Without no hesitation she put the candy bar, and jolly rancher in her pocket. She figured she'd steal the candy and keep all the money for herself.

She stepped outta line and begin walking towards the door . . . .

"Hey little girl wait, wait," the Arab lady said.

Latisha got nervous and tried to run outta the store.

A shot came from a .357 hit Latisha in the back.

Little Latisha never seen the gun, she just heard the shot, and felt the bullet. Her body couldn't take it she shook, and drop as the sound of the gun was like an echo as everyone in the store begin yelling, and screaming and running outta the store . . . .

The Arab man grabbed the gun from his wife.

"What made you do that," he asked? "I didn't do it purpose it was a mistake I pointed the gun at her just to scare her and it went off," the Arab lady said . . . .

The Arab man walked over and looked at the little girl lying there in her own blood. In his own silent mind he prayed to Allah that she wasn't dead. Swiftly visions of his very own little girl lying there shot and bleeding raced through his head . . . .

"I hope she aint dead," he said. "Go, go, get in the car and drive away," he said. "Where to," she asked? "Go to my friends Whola's house he got a private jet tell him to take you back to Saudia Arabia. Here take this gun to, and give it to Whola's and tell him I said dispose of it, he'll know what to do with it," he said . . . .

As she ran out the back door to her car, he ran to lock the front doors, and the back door behind her. He went to get all the surveillance videos, ran out the back door up the alley to throw the DVD's in the garbage, ran back into the store locked the back door swiftly.

Dialed 911 and told the police a little girl just got shot, and that he needed an ambulance right now. Little did he know someone had already called the police, they were already on their way.

Once the police and the paramedics arrived one paramedic checked Latisha's pulse and seen that she was still living.

Abdula felt a momentary sign of relief knowing that, that little girl was alive.

The ambulance rushed Latisha to the hospital.

He told the police his version of the story. Then they asked for the surveillance videos. He told them that he didn't have any because his surveillance system was broke.

The police continued to search for shell casings or any other type of physical evidence, none was found.

Some of the officer went outside across the street to the crowd, and got a statement for someone that was actually in the store when the incident occurred . . . .

After many hours searching for evidence the police escorted Abdula to the police station so he could file a police report. As they walked out the store once Abdula finished properly locking the front door they walked towards the police car as one female out of the crowd from across the street yelled out, "bitch I hope you die."

One black detective paused looked over at her curiously wondering why did she make that outburst.

So they continued on to the police station once they made it there it was seven other people there that was in the store when the shooting occurred getting reports filed.

The police surrounded Abdula and escorted him to the interrogation room way in the back. All the officers left him in the room by himself.

Through the glass Abdula seen all the officers talking amongst themselves he couldn't hear what they were saying through the door that was closed and that had real thick glass.

Abdula noticed how the big black officer face was in shock as the other officers talked.

Majority of the officers left the hallway and went to various areas in police station as the big black officer and a little short fat white officer stayed in the hallway talking.

Eventually the white officer spent off as the black officer entered the room smiling . . . .

"So you say three men was robbing your store, as the little girl tried to run out the door one of the men shot her in the back, correct," the black officer said. "Yes, that's correct," Abdula said. "Three black guys right," the black officer said. "Right," Abdula said.

The black officer started to smile harder than before . . . .

"We got eight people, one by the store, and seven people in station right now as we speak saying that your wife shot that lil girl," the black officer said. "That's a lie, why would my wife shoot a little girl," Abdula said . . . .

The black officer gave no reply but handcuffed Abdula . . . .

For hours different officers tried to get Abdula to tell the truth about what had happen but Abdula stuck to his story . . . .

Abdula was placed in a holding cell, as they went on a manhunt for his wife . . . .

Somebody went back and told everybody from the hood that Abdula told the police a lie that a nigga shot Latisha instead his wife. People from the hood begin to uproar . . . .

Later that night Latisha's auntie walk up with her heavy make-up damaged from a over flow of tears. She walked up to some the guys standing on the corner felt to her knees and begin crying loudly . . . .

"She didn't make it, God took my baby away from me," Latisha's aunt said . . . .

A lot of people from the hood including Latisha's family just blanked out. First they went to Abdula's store and set fire to it. Then they went to each every Arab business in the hood, and fucked them up, damn near killed two Arabs. Burning down all their businesses to the ground; they pour gasoline on one Arab and set him on fire, damn near killed him to, but he saved his own life by using the stop, drop, and roll method once they left . . . .

It was hard for the police to contain the violence that night . . . .

For a couple of days to follow people from the hood, as well as homicide would search for Abdula's wife, she was nowhere to be found . . . .

Three days after Latisha was shot, and killed Abdula was charged with conspiracy to commit murder. Homicide rigged it up as if he told his wife to do it . . . .

Abdula was sent to the county jail, and given a high bond because he was a flight risk. His bond was set at a hundred thousand to walk. A hundred thousand wasn't shit to him he owned other stores and a few apartment buildings. He bonded out the same day . . . .

About a week after Latisha was killed, and buried niggas from the hood was tired of looking for Abdula's wife, but became even thirstier to find Abdula's wife to take her life away as she did Latisha . . . .

It was this young nigga that was sixteen named Twon whom inner soul had been crying out since Latisha's death; he cried out feeling like why, why this little girl Latisha had to die . . . .

Unexpectedly Twon had heard that Abdula had a store on the other side of town . . . .

The next morning Twon, and two of his guys got strapped, and went to the store early in the morning before it even opened looking for Abdula's wife or one of Abdula's family members. To his surprise there Abdula was opening up his store, he couldn't believe it he thought Abdula was still in jail. They pulled up the block and parked . . . .

"Man let's just rush up on him, and make him show us where his wife is," Twon said. "Be for real you think he just gone tell us where his wife is at," Q said. "People tend to do a lot of things that they wouldn't normally do once they got a big ass gun in their face," Twon said. "He aint gonna tell you where his wife at," John, John said with confidence. "We still gotta try," Twon said. "Fam, it's broad daylight man, you just wanna walk up and up guns on him," Q said. "What the fuck did we get strapped and come over here for," Twon ask? "We need to stake out the store first," John, John said.

"You sound like a nerdy college motherfucker, one of them white boys, we need to stake out the store first. You niggas is stupid, we come all the way over here to gets down and you niggas act like ya'll scared. This nigga wife done killed this little girl, shot her to death for no reason. That's one thing about death aint no coming back from that shit once you die it's over. You know what, fuck ya'll niggas, on my life," Twon said . . . .

Twon bailed out of the car walked up to Abdula upped on him made him finish opening up the store walked him in made him get on his knees, slid his throat with a razor then shot him in the head once execution style and left the store.

Twon came running out the store with the razor in his left hand, and the gun in his right hand, bailed in the car pulled off . . . .

As they rode, destination to the hood Q and John, John remained silent as Twon talked and kicked it like nothing never happen . . . .

In reality Twon was going to walk Abdula into the store to force him to tell him where his wife was at, and for him to take him to his wife; but once he got in the store visions of Latisha laying in a casket begin flashing in his head which provoked him to take away Abdula's life . . . .

A couple of weeks later Twon was having a small birthday party for his seventeen birthday at a tavern in the hood. Outta nowhere homicide rushed in placed him under arrest Twon had no idea of what was going on, and he wondered to himself which murder were they grabbing him for cuz he had been doing so much dirt. He would've never guessed that it was the murder of Abdula . . . .

Homicide probably would've never grabbed or even suspected him over that murder if Q and John, John wouldn't never went back to hood and told people. Q and John, John only told a few people, but those few people told a few more people, and those few more people told a few people and word of mouth slowly spreaded . . . .

Some nigga from the hood was getting hassled from the police for some other shit, and gave up information about Twon killing Abdula so they would let him free. The police didn't ask the nigga about any unsolved murders, but he knew that if he gave them that lead that they'd definitely let him go and forget about the petty shit they was harassing him for, and it worked . . . .

Once they made it to the police station Twon came to find out they had a witness whom lived across the street from the store seen him and that they had surveillance from the store that showed him killing Abdula. What Twon didn't know was that by him having his hoody on with the strings slightly tied around his mouth, and had his head down majority of the time during the incident that the witness nor the surveillance really couldn't actually say, or show it was him . . . .

They put Twon in a line up in order for the one witness to positively I.D. him, and she did point him out that was only because he was a real short guy, everybody else in the lineup was tall.

Twon always thought line ups were only in movies but he came to see that the police do that for real . . . .

They shipped Twon to the county and charged him with Abdula's murder. Gave him a high ass bond so Twon knew he wasn't going to bond out . . . .

This was Twon first time to the county he had only been to juvenile detention once now that he was seventeen there was no more juvenile for him he had to be with the grown men.

Once he made it to the Cook county jail, division 10 he was screened to see if he was gang affiliated, he was an UnderTaker ViceLord. He got introduced to the other ViceLords, they gave him a little cosmetics, and food. They offered squares, but he didn't smoke. Afterwards they laid out to him the security measurements . . . .

His first day on the deck was average . . . .

Twon immediately noticed that the county was totally different from the juvenile detention center in many different ways . . . .

On his third day of being in jail he awoke from the sounds the doors being unlocked to eat breakfast . . . .

I can't believe I'm stuck in jail for a body, he thought to his self as he walked to go get his tray . . . .

They had scrambled eggs and oatmeal on the trays. This was his first time eating oatmeal, it was a bomb to him . . . .

In juvenile they'd go to the lunchroom to eat as school kids did, in the Cook county jail there was no lunchroom in his division, the officers brought the trays to the deck, and two or three assigned inmates passed the trays out to the rest of the people on the deck.

Certain inmates would get special trays that revolved around health issues; like hypro trays, and low fat trays . . . .

Twon ate his tray went in cell in attempts to go back to sleep . . . .

Approximately three minutes after Twon laid off in the bunk he heard one nigga say the next time you bitches don't give me my hypro tray we gonna tear this bitch up.

Then one of the niggas that was working the trays yelled out it aint gonna be no next time and hit him in his mouth for calling him a bitch.

In 0.3 seconds the deck went up, he kicked off a riot between the fin ball, and niggas under the six. The fin ball consists of mainly ViceLords, Latin Kings, and Black P-Stones, amongst others. The six mainly consist of G.D's, B.D's, and Latin Folks amongst others.

Twon begin to hear people yelling, the bottom of gym shoes squeaking against the floor.

He jumped out his top bunk to see what was going on, and seen food trays flying back and forth, knives penetrated flesh, as others were getting stumped, and beat . . . .

Twon was on his way out of the cell, but in 0.3 seconds they niggas under the six, and the niggas under the fin separated, both to each side of the deck, as a standoff.

Twon then seen more knives than he'd seen in kitchen sets . . . .

Twon cell was in the back where the niggas under six was so he didn't know what to do, he hoped they didn't run in there on him . . . .

Within no time a gang of C/O's ran on the deck to disperse the violence . . . .

Everybody that had knives tossed them to the ground and ran to their cells as the C/O's came in whupping nigga's and locking them in their cells. All those that were injured remained out there cells until the paramedics came from the med unit of the county . . . .

Nigga's from both sides got fucked up real bad, from puncher lungs, to broken jaws, to staples in heads, to stitches in faces . . . .

The C/O's found twelve knives . . . .

Twon had heard many bad things about the county before he even made it there, but he never knew that a deck would go up, and niggas get fucked up real bad over a petty hypro tray . . . .

What Twon didn't know was that the individual working the trays gave the man three regular trays and apologized for not giving him a hypro tray, they gave his tray away to someone else by mistake. The man accepted there apology ate the three regular trays and started talking shit.

This was like a welcoming party to the county jail for Twon . . . .

They officer in division 10 decided to split up the deck before they let them off lock down.

When they moved him to another deck he was placed in a cell with a Latin King; which was good for him because Latin Kings and ViceLords were under the fin, allies.

His new celly was nicknamed Loco and he lived up to his name. Twon and Loco hit it off immediately.

The division 10 was still on lock down. Each time someone on any deck got stabbed the entire division would go on lockdown. Twon hadn't got in touch with his family yet because each time he'd call he'd get no answer. Now that he was on lock down he couldn't call at all.

Loco had been locked up for two years fighting a murder. During those two years Loco had caught all type of assaults on inmates, aggravated batteries for stabbing inmates, and UUW for getting caught with a knife. Loco was the true essence of a gang banger.

As days past Town begin to open up to Loco and tell his story of why he was locked up. Loco took a liking for him knowing that he wasn't a stool penguin to work with the police and sign a statement on John-John, and Q. Loco knew he could've made all three of them rapy's on Abdula's murder, but he kept his mouth shut.

Loco had a personal vendetta for stool penguins, because his rapy was turning states on him . . . .

"Don't worry about your case, just pray to the creator and leave it in his hands. One of the best things to do while you're in her is read. Reading can take your mind into different areas. It's been times where I been reading a book, and forgot I was even in jail, it was like I was one of the characters in the book, real talk," Loco said. "What kind of books should I read," Town asked? "I read almost anything I can get my hands on, me and you two different people, maybe you should read whatever books that's exciting to you, the ones that keep your mind away from the free world. I got a book for you to read, read this," Loco said as he reached under his mattress grabbed a book and handt it to him.

Twon read the title to himself, The Greatest Sex Stories Ever, Volume 1.

"I don't want to read no sex stories," Twon said. "Go ahead this shit a bomb," Loco said . . . .

Twon got on the top bunk opened up the book and started reading it: Chapter 1, Several People . . . .

Chad and Felicia was a married couple that had been happily married for twenty years. Chad was 43, and Felicia was 50 years of age. Throughout their twenty years of marriage they didn't have too many problems; not once did Chad or Felicia unfaithfully cheat on one another.

Chad and Felicia sex life was average, but they both wanted more excitement . . . .

Chad worked in an office building around many women, but he'd grew a liking for this eighteen year old young lady that had been working there for only a few months. Her name was Rita. Rita had one of the nicest ass any man would love. Each day at work she'd either wear tight jeans, or a full length tight skirt. On top of her nice ass she had a cute baby doll face. Each day Chad and Rita would conversate, but nothing outta the ordinary, simply casual conversation.

One day Rita and Chad's conversation begin to get a little heated. Rita begin to tell Chad that she'd only been sexually active with one man in her life, her last boyfriend.

By Chad being faithful to his wife he got on to another topic. But in the back of Chad's mind he knew that when a woman told a man such business that was because she was interested in him . . . .

Twon liked the story, and couldn't put the book down, wanted to see what would happen next, so he continued to read . . . .

Felicia would go grocery shopping most of the time by herself. She became acquainted with a young man named Micheal that worked at the grocery store.

Micheal was 22 years old and one of the most hansom man Felicia had ever laid eyes upon.

Felicia and Micheal would have casual conversation when she came to the grocery store, but nothing outta the ordinary.

One day when Felicia was leaving the grocery store Micheal told her that she had a nice ass. Felicia couldn't believe what he'd said. She turned around and asked him "what did you just say." "I said you got a nice ass." She begin laughing, and thanked him for the compliment . . . .

Later on that night Felicia and Chad was watching some stand-up comedy on TV. One of the comedians begin talking about how this younger lady was attracted to him, and of course he made a joke out of it. Chad begin to tell Felicia about that young lady from work that liked him. Felicia begin to tell Chad about the young man from the grocery store that liked her. It was no big deal to either one of them because they had a marriage built of trust.

Before the night end they watched a XXX rated movie. The movie consist of all threesomes. Chad told Felicia he'd like to be involved in a threesome. Felicia told Chad she might if she wasn't married. She didn't want to see her husband having sex with another woman . . . .

After the movie they sexed throughout the night . . . .

The next day at work Rita was all over Chad. Chad was intelligent enough to know she wanted sex . . . . Coincidently on the same exact day Micheal gave Felicia a hug at the grocery store. This wasn't a average hug, this hug was a hug as it was from one lover to another . . . .

Later that day both Felicia and Chad told each other of their experience with the youngsters. Chad admitted to Felicia that he liked Rita, but could never get involved while he was married to her. Felicia said she felt the same way about Micheal.

Out of nowhere Chad said let's invite them to our bedroom one by one. Felicia begin to blush, while giggling and said no in a phony way. Chad had been with her all these years and knew her no wasn't sincere.

Chad didn't say anything else about a threesome for several days . . . .

Within the next several days at work Chad begin to get physical with Rita. He even palmed her ass and titties she enjoyed it.

What Rita didn't understand was why he didn't want to creep off and have sex; Chad didn't want to cheat on his wife, the times he palmed her ass and titties was when his dick got hard and he got out of control . . . .

A day later after he palmed her merchandise they was at work talking about various things. Out of nowhere Chad kissed Rita. After kissing her he told her that he wanted her but didn't want to cheat on his wife. She told him what she don't know won't hurt her . . . .

Twon begin to really get excited, thinking to himself that they should make a movie out of this shit . . . .

"I just can't cheat on my wife. I even told her about you and she'd enjoy meeting you. The only way you and I could get together was in a threesome," Chad said.

Chad paused hoping she'd say she wanted to have a threesome that would've been like a dream come true for Chad. As he paused she paused, confused not knowing how to reply . . . .

"Well in order for me to have a threesome I'd really have to like the man a whole lot to involve myself in that," Rita said. "Do you really like me," Chad asked? Rita begin to smirk. "You got a valid point because I really do like you a lot. I like that you don't want to cheat on your wife, most men wouldn't turn down pussy married or not. First let me meet your wife and we will see how it goes," Rita said . . . .

Chad went straight home from work. When he got there Felicia was naked ready for sex, and he gave her sex, great sex . . . .

After sexing Chad told Felicia all that happen between Rita and himself he left out the part when he palmed her ass and titties. Felicia told him she didn't know about a threesome . . . .

As days passed along Chad continued to ask Felicia of a threesome. She told him that if we have a threesome it would have to be with another man. Chad told her to let's try it with Rita first . . . .

"You'd let your wife have sex with another woman," Felicia asked? "Yes if I'm involved," Chad said . . . .

Felicia remained silent for a little while . . . .

"Forget it let's give it a try with Rita, but if I don't like it I'm not doing it anymore," Felicia said . . . .

The next day at work Chad told Rita, "My wife wants to have a threesome with you." "How do you know that she don't even know me," Rita said. "Although she don't know you I've been telling her good things about you. We've been together for twenty years and my wife and I are in love, therefore we do what it takes to make each other happy. This threesome will make all three of us happy," Chad said . . . .

Later on that day Chad showed up at his home with Rita. Dinner was already ready. All three sat down and ate dinner. While eating dinner Rita and Felicia begin to conversate about girl things, they seemed to be getting along well.

"You look nice," Felicia said to Rita. "I was thinking the same thing about you," Rita said . . . .

At that very moment Chad knew that they wanted to get it in.

Chad went into the living room and placed on a XXX rated movie; of course the movie was of a sexual threesome. He then called both women in to watch the movie.

To his surprise as they begin watching the movie the girls acted like they couldn't take their eyes off of it . . . .

In the process of Chad and the girls watching the movie Chad spontaneously upped his dick and told Felicia to suck it. Felicia begin sucking it like never before. It was as she'd studied the art of deep throating.

As Rita sat and watched she was amazed of how long his dick was. Rita was afraid to have his big dick in her little pussy.

As Felicia continued sucking on his dick she looked out the corner of her eyes to see Rita's facial expression. Rita's facial expression looked as if in the back of her mind she was saying hurry up bitch I'm next.

In no time flat Chad begin to bust a nut, he released it in Felicia's face; at that very moment it was as Rita felt like she was releasing her orgasm . . . .

"Take them panties off," Chad said in a low firm, sensual tone of voice . . . .

The women didn't say a word as Rita laid on the couch Felicia snatched of Rita's pants, then her panties, then her shirt, and bra. Then Felicia laid on the couch as Rita snatched of all her clothes . . . .

They both were ready to eat away at each other's pussy but Chad told Felicia to get on all fours. Chad banged Felicia pussy as Rita watched Felicia continuously licked her tongue in and out at Rita while hollering unable to take the dick as usual . . . .

Chad stop fucking Felicia and told Rita to get on all fours. As he stuck his dick in her she tried to run from it, Felicia held Rita's hands down, as Chad gripped her waist tightly and started slamming his dick in, and out the pussy. Chad couldn't believe how good, wet, and tight her pussy was. As Rita was hollering Felicia continued to hold her hands down, and kissed her in the mouth, as their tongue connected Rita could feel herself cumming . . . .

Felicia stop kissing her, but continued to hold her hands down as Rita looked at Felicia with her eyes slightly open breathing heavily, and moaning saying, "oh his dick is too big, his dick is too big, his dick is too big." Felicia kissed her again, and then told her, "Just take it baby."

Chad started banging Rita even harder because he was getting ready to nut, and Rita knew this . . . .

"Please take it out, and nut my mouth," Rita said . . . .

Chad took it out, but before he could put his dick in her mouth his nut splashed all across her lips. She liked the nut off her lips, and then licked the nut off his dick, and set on the couch as he stood straight up she begin sucking his dick.

Her mouth is fantastic, Chad thought to himself.

As Rita continued sucking on his dick she could feel Felicia sucking on her titties, and trying stick her hand up her pussy, as Rita tried to control Felicia's hand, as Chad was force feeding her his dick she felt overpowered and bullied, and she loved it . . . .

Then Chad started eating Rita's pussy while Felicia sucked on his dick, as Felicia fingered her own self all at the same time.

We should've been done a threesome, Felicia thought to herself . . . .

Then Chad begin eating Felicia's pussy while she ate Rita's pussy, all at the same time . . . .

Before they even begun sexing Chad just knew that at least one of the girls wouldn't cooperate with some of the sexual acts, oh how he was wrong.

Then Rita got on her knees to suck Chad's dick again while Felicia finger fucked Rita's pussy, and ass at the same time . . . .

Chad was really enjoying himself, but the girls were enjoying themselves even more . . . .

All night Felicia, Chad, and Rita sexed thoroughly . . . .

The next morning all three got into the shower together. Afterwards Felicia went to work. Chad took Rita to her house to change clothes, and then Chad and Rita went to work . . . .

All day at work they gazed into each other's eyes with lust built within . . . .

After work he hugged her and told her he'd sat up a date when Felicia, her, and him could hang out, even if she didn't want to sex again. He told her the date would probably be tomorrow.

Both Rita and Chad was in a hurry so they immediately went their separate ways . . . .

He rushed home from work hoping Felicia was there. He wanted to privately ask her how much she enjoyed intercourse last night . . . .

Once he made it from work she was there. Soon as he walked through the door she begin tongue kissing him like never before.

Afterwards they sat down, and talked . . . .

"How did you enjoy the experience last night," he asked? "Last night was wonderful let's do it again tonight," she said . . . .

He begin to smile knowing that he'd open up this wonderful door of group sex at its best . . . .

"No we aint going to do it tonight, let's wait a few days, we don't want to seem too eager," he said . . . .

Right then and there she begin tongue kissing him, and they undressed and fucked for hours . . . .

Later on that night Felicia begin to tell him about her secret freaky desires. The one freaky desire that fascinated him the most was when she told him she wanted to have sex with a group of only men as they treated her like a cheap hooker. He begin thinking to himself like damn I'm married to a closet freak. He felt good that he'd brought the freaky side outta her . . . .

The next day at work he walked up to Rita and hugged her liked he hadn't seen her in years, and was happy to see her . . . .

"Did you enjoy yourself the other night," Chad asked Rita? "Yes I did I aint never felt that good before," Rita said. "Which part did you like the best," Chad asked? "I liked it the best when you, and your wife was taking turns performing oral sex on me, but actually I liked all of it, but when you and her took turns performing oral sex it was a little better than all the rest. I wanted to tell you yesterday, but we didn't do too much talking yesterday," Rita said. "Yeah I felt the same way but I believe that when you and my wife took turns sucking my dick that was the best part for me," Chad said. "Sshhhh, you don't have talk all loud we don't want anybody in our business," Rita said. "Sorry about that," Chad said . . . .

She then kissed him on the cheek and said, "Thanks for bringing me to life the other night. When are we going to do it again," she asked? "Honestly me and my wife enjoy having you around without sex, but we'd love to have sex with you more often, but it's only one problem," he said as he looked out the window in order for her not to be looking at him face to face. "What's the problem," she asked? "Me and my wife wants you to do everything sexually," he said. "Sure it's not a problem," she said . . . .

Chad came at her like that to insure that he could have his way with her this time and every other time . . . .

"Once our day at work is over I'll take you home with me," Chad told her. "Okay that's cool," Rita said . . . .

Chad and Rita showed up at Chad's home unexpectedly. As they entered the door Felicia couldn't believe it she became overjoyed, instantly smiling and undressing. In 0.7 seconds Felicia was totally naked tongue kissing Rita.

Chad and Rita then undressed. Chad ordered Felicia to suck his dick. Rita just stood there naked watching.

Within minutes Chad bust a nut in Felicia face. He then ordered Rita to suck his dick; she acted like she didn't want to do it, but she got on her knees and did it anyway . . . .

Chad grabbed the back of her head and begin fucking her face, once he got ready to nut he released it in her mouth.

Chad stood Rita up bent her over and begin fucking her from the back. Chad liked Rita's pussy, it was much tighter than Felicia pussy. While Chad fucked Rita from the back giving her the dick in the hardest rawest format Felicia stood up watching while fingering her own pussy with her index, and middle finger while sucking on two of her fingers from the other hand.

When it was time for Chad to release his enormous load of nut he let it loose on Rita's ass cheeks as he jagged all of the nut of his dick . . . .

As Twon continued to read the book he begin to think to himself like damn this shit better than a porn movie. Loco was right reading a good book takes your mind away from being in jail.

The book was so good that Twon actually felt like he was living it himself. He felt like he was married to Felicia, and at that very moment he was the one busting nuts on Rita's ass cheeks.

Twon dick was harder than it ever been reading that sex story . . . .

Loco laid on the bottom bunk remaining silent knowing what Twon was experiencing off reading the book. Loco knew that this book captivated readers, because the sex scenes were incredible . . . .

Twon continued to read . . . .

"Felicia lay on the couch, now Rita stick your tongue as deep in her pussy as you can," Chad said . . . .

She stuck her tongue in Felicia's pussy, and started eating . . . .

While she was eating it Chad whispers in Rita's ear . . . .

"Rita you're doing a great job I'm proud of you. Me and my wife loves you," Chad said . . . .

Of course Rita knew they didn't really love her but she still liked hearing it . . . .

"Yes, yes keep eating that pussy just like that," Chad said while fingering Rita's pussy . . . .

Chad stops fingering Rita and started eating her pussy.

After Rita came twice Chad stuck his dick off in her which made her eat Felicia's pussy even better . . . .

After Rita was done eating Felicia's pussy, and Chad was done fucking Rita, Chad sat on the couch to relax and take a break. The girls didn't want a break. Rita begin sucking on Chad's dick while Felicia was licking on the crack of Rita's ass . . . .

After sexing for hours all three showered together and then Felicia and Chad dropped Rita off at home . . . .

A few days later Felicia begin to ask about Rita because it had been a few days since the last time she'd seen her, and she'd wanted to fuck her again.

Chad would see Rita at work every day, but figured he'd wait a week or two before he brought her home again Chad and Rita had got real close, they'd even start going on lunch breaks together . . . .

One day while at the grocery store Felicia wasn't even thinking about Micheal, and outta nowhere he approached her looking good as ever. He had a smile on face that would light up the world, and that particular day he'd been to the barber shop . . . .

"You look good with your new haircut," Felicia said. "Thought I'd try a new look. I haven't seen you shopping in a few days," Micheal said. "That's because I didn't need any groceries until today. How are you doing," she asked? "Well I'm doing alright, tired of this job at the grocery store," he said. "You know you gotta do what you gotta do to pay the bills," she said. "Yeah you right about that," Micheal said . . . .

"You starting to get thick," Micheal said. "That's your second time making a comment about my ass, keep your eyes off my body parts, I'm married," she said. "But you do have a nice body," he said. "Thanks," she said.

"I can't lie I cherish the moments we share together when you come to the grocery store. Each day I watch the front doors in hopes of you entering one of them. My day isn't complete unless I see you," Micheal said. "Is that right," she said. "To keep it real I wish we could be together all day every day. They stood in the aisle of the grocery store and talked for almost an hour non-stop.

After an hour she purchased her grocerys, as Micheal escorted her to her car . . . .

Before she knew it she was in Micheal's apartment getting fucked . . . .

After having sex with Micheal she felt bad that she cheated on her husband. She started to tell Mike how she was feeling inside . . . .

"Mike I'd been with this man for twenty years and not once did I cheat on him until you came along," she said. "But at least it was with someone who cares about you. He'll never find out about us if things get deeper," Mike said. "It's not the point of him finding out it's the fact that I did cheat on him," she said . . . .

Felicia laid on Mike's bed with her hand over her face. Mike assumed she was crying, but she wasn't. She was hiding her shame, while mentally going through a thing.

Mike started to eat her pussy to make her feel better, and it worked . . . .

Later that day Felicia moped around the house . . . .

"What's wrong you aint been your normal self, all day," Chad said. "It's nothing wrong, I feel good actually," Felicia said. "Stop it, I been knowing you all these years, and I know when something is wrong with you," Chad said. "There's nothing wrong," Felicia said with confidence . . . . Chad knew she was lying . . . .

For days Felicia walked around feeling sad . . . .

Chad knew something was wrong, he decided to take her out to eat, and to a dance club, Felicia loved to dance . . . .

Once they made it back home Chad hugged Felicia, and held her in his arms, and told her that he loved her, which made Felicia feel even worser . . . .

Felicia went into the back room and came right back out . . . .

"I love you, and wouldn't ever want to lose you," Felicia said. "Don't won't too lose me," Chad said. "I got a secret to tell you," Felicia said. "Aw that's why you been all sad for the last few days," Chad said. "It's a problem with me telling you my secret, I don't want to be handt no divorce papers," Felicia said. "I'm your husband you can talk to me about anything," Chad said. "I didn't play fair ball I cheated," Felicia said. "With who," Chad said. "The young guy at the grocery store," She said. "I knew that, that's why you been all sad, and that's why you ask me earlier, what would I do if I was married to a woman and caught her cheating. Well I gotta secret to I been cheating on you with Rita," Chad said . . . .

Chad began hugging her tightly . . . .

"I can't believe you're not mad," Felicia said. "Actually I'm glad I married someone like you, how many women you know that would cheat, and then come tell their husband about it, how many women you know that would have a threesome with their husband," Chad said. "Where's Rita," Felicia asked?

Chad began laughing knowing Felicia wanted action . . . .

"I'll bring her over tomorrow," Chad said. "Thank you, I really need, and want her," Felicia said. "Do you want to have sex with the guy from the grocery store again," Chad asked . . . Felicia paused before answering the question . . . . She looked Chad in his eyes, and said yep. Chad gave no remarked, instead he just smiled.

The next day he brought Rita home both Rita and Felicia was so happy to see one another that most of the night they had sex with only one another like he wasn't even there . . . .

The next day freaky thoughts begin racing through his head . . . .

"What's the guy named that work at the grocery store," Chad asked? "His name Micheal, I just call him Mike," she said. "Why don't we invite him, and Rita over for dinner, then we can have a foursome," Chad said . . . .

Felicia begin smiling, and laughing . . . .

"A foursome I never heard of that before, I can invite him, but I don't know if he'll be interested in coming," she said. "He will be interested in having sex with two women at the same time, trust me," Chad said. "So you going to have sex with another man," Felicia asked? "Hell naw, me and him gone have sex with you, and Rita," Chad said. "Okay I'll go to the grocery store tomorrow to ask him," she said. "Don't you have his phone number," Chad asked? "No," she said. "You rotate with a guy, having sexual intercourse with him, and you don't have his number," Chad said. "No, I only sex with him once when we rotate with each other it's always when I come to the grocery store, I'll see him at the grocery store tomorrow, and I'll ask him," Rita said . . . .

The next day Chad, and Rita was in Chad's kitchen preparing dinner. All the while, while they were cooking they hoped that Felicia would bring Mike home for the foursome. As the food was done cooking, still nice, and hot they laid it out on the table like a Thanksgiving dinner.

Chad and Felicia didn't eat they waited for Mike and Rita. They just sat at the table reminiscing . . . .

About forty five minutes after the food was done, to Chad, and Rita's surprise in comes Felicia, and Mike. Chad, and Rita was so happy that they jumped straight up out their chairs hugging Mike one by one as if they'd known him all their lives . . . .

They sat down, and began to eat dinner, as the four of them continued to smile with nasty sexual thoughts running through their heads . . . .

Felicia got up went to the bathroom, and came back naked as the day she was born. Mike mouth drop knowing it was time for action . . . .

Chad stood up upped his dick, Felicia got on her knees and began sucking his dick. Mike stood up and watched in amazement . . . .

Rita got on her knees unzipped Mikes pants, he stuffed his dick in her mouth as she begin sucking on it as if it was a lolly pop . . . .

Mike watched his own dick go in and out of Rita's mouth feeling the joyous pleasure of what sex brings within this life . . . .

Her mouth is fantastic, Mike thought to himself.

Mike continued to glance over at Felicia's performance and couldn't wait to get a piece of her.

Outta nowhere Mike felt his dick get harder as the nut exploded in Rita's mouth as Rita swallowed all of it like a champ.

Mike couldn't believe Rita made him nut it was hard for a woman to suck his dick and make him nut . . . .

Mike walked over to Felicia and stood her up, as she was now on her feet bent over still sucking Chad's dick Mike stuffed his dick in her pussy, and begin fucking the shit out of her . . . .

As they could hear Felicia slightly moaning although Chad dick was on her mouth, Rita begin playing with her own pearl tongue, and started sucking Felicia titties nipples one by one . . . .

I can't believe I got a dick in my pussy, a dick in my mouth, and another woman sucking my titties all at the same time, Felicia thought to herself.

Felicia kept cumming back to back hoping that all three wouldn't ever stop . . . .

Felicia opened her eyes looking up at Chad, as she felt Chads dick getting harder she knew he was getting ready to nut so she took his dick out of her mouth and begged him to nut in her face, and he nutted in her mouth and face . . . .

Mike laid Felicia on the couch on her back wanting more of that pussy he held her legs in the air and started stuffing his dick in and out of it . . . .

"Get on all fours on the floor," Chad told Rita . . . .

Chad stuffed his dick in Rita hard and fast as if he was made at the world, and she loved it. Chad worked the pussy, while she played with her own pearl tongue desiring to cum quicker and more pleasurable, and she did a great job of it . . . .

Chad told Rita to lie on her back on the floor, as his commence to tonguing and sucking her pussy. Mike stop fucking Felicia to eat Rita's pussy after Chad. Then Felicia ate Rita's pussy after Mike . . . .

Mike laid on the floor and both girls started sucking his dick at the same time, as Chad started taking turns fucking both girls from the back . . . .

As Mike nut came out he let it go in Felicia face and mouth. Then the girls started kissing each other as Chad continued stuffing his dick in and out of Felicia's pussy . . . .

After sex that night they showered and Mike drove Rita home . . . .

After that night Chad and Felicia did foursomes with Mike and Rita, and sometimes threesomes with Rita, and sometimes threesomes with just Mike . . . .

About nine months after that night Felicia, and Mike got married, and their marriage turned out to be a happy one . . . .

"Loco this book is a bomb fam," Twon said. "I knew you'd like it that's why I gave it to you, reading a good book takes your mind off bullshit," Loco said. "I only read chapter one, but it was hot, I couldn't stop reading it," Twon said. "I know that's why I gave it to you. I got a gang of books for you to read. I only read erotica when I'm alone. I mainly read nonfiction, and spiritual guidance books. I'm finna go to sleep so I want to cut the light off man, so can you wait to tomorrow to do some more reading," Loco said. "Yeah I'm cool on the light, you can cut it off," Twon said.

Twon laid back on the top bunk with constant visions of Rita, and Felicia having threesome with him. Twon dick stayed hard for hours, it was like he had popped some Viagra or something . . . .

CHAPTER 2

A few days later they were let off lock down Twon was able to get through to his family; they were happy to hear from him and disappointed that he was locked up for a murder. They immediately start sending money orders and religious pamphlets amongst other things. They were anxious for visiting day to come so they could come see him . . . .

Once visiting day came Twon, and everybody on the deck was preparing for visiting day.

Twon got quite a few visits from family members and friends showing love and support. They all promised that they'll always be there through the trials and tribulations of his case.

At the end of the day Twon last visitor showed up; it was his four month old pregnant girlfriend . . . .

Tears ran down her face in the visiting room as she cried out to Twon because she needed him there for support, and she knew that Twon wouldn't be there when the baby was born.

Twon left the visit early sad and confused knowing he wouldn't be there when the baby was born . . . .

Once he made it on the deck Loco could look at him and see and feel the sadness . . . .

Shortly after Twon's last visit they C/O's yelled out, "lock up time."

Once Twon and Loco made it within their cells Loco begin fixing burritos . . . .

"You think we should hook up all meat burritos, or this pasta I saved from dinner," Loco asked? "It don't matter," Twon said. "What's wrong, why you looking all sad for," Loco asked? "My girl on visits crying, talking about she can't do it without me, and that my baby gone be born without his daddy there, everything she said was the truth, sometimes the truth hurt, and it really hurted," Twon said. "Man, you got a body you might be fighting for two or three years, and then get found guilty, and gotta work on appeals. I understand how you feel because I got kids to, but you got a body man you gotta get with the program. I know I aint gone never see the streets again I got to many cases, my rapy turned states, and I done caught gang of cases since I been in here and I might catch some more. But I don't let shit get me down I keep my head up to the sky, and just keep, keeping on. I must admit I aint been to church in a long time but I do pray to God; what you need to do is pray, theirs power in prayer," Loco said. "I got to do some reading tonight. How long you gone be with them burritos," Twon asked? "Be patient they'll be ready in no time, let the young chef work his magic," Loco said, as they both begin laughing . . . .

"Damn these burritos is a bomb, what you put on them some Mexican dip or some shit," Twon said as they begin laughing. "Naw that some homemade bar-b-que sauce," Loco said. "Whatever it is it's a bomb," Twon said . . . .

I wonder what I'm going to read tonight. I can't read no sex stories while Loco in the cell with me them sex stories to hot, Twon thought to his self as he continued eating his burrito . . . .

Loco reached under his bunk and went in his brown paper bag filled with books, and pulled out a book that was average size in length but small in width. The book was only a hundred pages. He handt the book to Twon . . . .

"What kind of book is this," Twon asked as he reached for the book. "This a book poetry, it aint regular poetry it's called ghetto poetry it's kind of like handwritten rap mixed with hardcore open mic poetry, you'll like it trust me," Loco said.

Twon looked at the cover of the book, it looked like the cover of a rap C.D. He seen this little short big head bald head dude, with a black, and gray fur vest on the cover, which was the author. He read the title ghetto poetry by Flame.

"What kind of name is Flame," Twon asked? "It's not his real name, some authors use a pen name just like how rappers use different names, some authors do the same," Loco said. "I don't want to read no poetry," Twon said as he tried to hand him the book back. "Read it you'll like, remember when I gave you the sex stories you was acting the same way, then when you start reading it you feel in love," Loco said . . . .

Twon didn't respond but instantly got on the top bunk, and began reading the book. He skipped through the acknowledgements and went straight to the first page and began reading:

1
New

On the new investigated to see if black and gold, red and black or
black and blue. Visions never knew the goodness of the truth.
We were self-made kings, and queens, and humanized gurus.
Never knew it was designed for the black beauties to improve.
Lost and confused a minute issue was overdue.
Stabbed up a hundred something times, by his own multitude.
A fool sacrifice his own life, tossed away like rotten fruit . . . .
He never knew, never growed, never grew.
That poem was decent, Twon thought to
himself, as he decided to read more:

2
Friends

Friends that was once friends changed on me in the
end. Literally murdered my uncle, my next of kin,
while I resided in the belly of the beast within.
To his killer they be-friend.
In God we trust, not men.
Fake tears at funeral, basement tattoos on skin.
Open up on his joint claimed it as their own land.
Sexed his girlfriend.
Once I was released they walked up to me to
shake my hand as nothing never happen.
In the beginning and the end problems
occurred through my so called friends.

3
A Way To Live A Way To Die
Pitiful Cries.
Whip away tears from eyes.
Knowing that it's heaven above the skies when we die.
First you must be baptized, free from all sinful ties,
be a product of Godly things in others eyes.
Speak the truth not a lie.
Use scriptures to abide by the Lords
guide, and as a way to survive.
Worship God until you die.

4
Love and Hate
It's a thin line between love and hate.
Be careful, watch for chameleon of snakes,
even your homies, and ones you date.
Demons that made the creator close heavens
gates, enemy of the states.
Control fate.
Be careful not to cross that thin line between love and hate
where firely sparks have already set a date, sealed fate.
Kill and take.
Love and hate.

5
She Wanted To Fly
She said she wanted to soar like a bald eagle, so high.
I asked her how high.
She said she wanted to reach the sky.
She really believe she could fly, she literally wanted
to touch the sky one day before she die.
She sat by looking out her project window smoking a dip
cigarette to get high with no hesitation jumped out of the
window saying, "I can fly, I can fly, I can fly," right before
her skull hit the ground cracking open a thousand times.
She wanted to fly a suicidal way to die.
Could never be forgiving for that suicidal sin

she had to try, no heaven in the sky.
Her soul shall forever burn in eternal fire.
Right before she die, she wanted to fly.

"Loco, these ghetto poems cool, who put you up on these," Twon asked? "A lot of people know about Flame he from the streets, I heard the nigga did fifteen straight for attempt murders. The niggas that use to work for him fucked up some money, and he fucked them up, and they got down on him in court. While he was in jail he wrote a gang of books then he got out, he got them published and got rich," Loco said. "Straight up?" "Yep. I heard he was one of them Travelers from off California, and Flournoy," Loco said. "Aw yeah," Twon said. "How long you gone be with the light man, I'm about ready to go to sleep," Loco said. "I wanna finish reading this book it won't take long. Soon as I get finished I'll cut the light off," Twon said. "Hurry up, nigga," Loco said, as he laid on the bottom bunk putting the blanket over his head . . . .

Twon continued to read the book, it seemed as each individual poem got even better each time he flipped to another page . . . .

In no time Twon finished the book hit the light, and laid on his bunk. It was hard for Twon to go straight to sleep because they were hollering out the doors for hours. He couldn't wait until they shut the fuck up . . . .

The next day the deck went up Loco stabbed a nigga in his eye for making that noise while he was trying to sleep the night before in return Loco was stabbed five times in the back, Twon got stabbed once in the hand, and others from both side the fin and the six got fucked up real bad . . . .

Loco was sent to the outside hospital. Once released from the hospital he was sent to seg with Twon amongst a bunch of others, some had went to the health care part of the county jail. Loco caught a new case which was nothing to him.

Twon and Loco stayed in seg. For thirty days. When they got out they were placed on the same deck, but not the same cell . . . .

This time Twon was smart he found a way to get a hold to some knives for security purposes. The ViceLords on that deck had plenty knives but he wanted his own for protection . . . .

The next day after Twon was released from seg. it was Twon's first court date. He went and met his public defender for the first time. His public defender was an African he hadn't look over any of Twons evidence yet, but scheduled the next court date to the next month . . . .

Twon made it to the deck, and his celly was on a special out of town visit, so Twon decided to ease his mind by reading a sex story . . . .

Twon begin reading this erotica book called Sexy Love, it was a book he got from Loco the day before . . . . Chapter 1

Starving Artist

Here I was a twenty seven year old starving artist . . . .

All through high school I tried to figure out what I'd major in once I started college. Well it wasn't anything that I'd like to build a career in; until my senior year in high school.

In my senior year of high school I begin to visit art galleries with one of my friends and I really begin to take a liking in art . . . .

I started to read stories about ancient artist. One of the main things I liked about some of the artist, that they would paint portraits that wouldn't look like anything in particular, and they wouldn't make any sense to the eyes of the beholder, but the public still loved them.

After I graduated high school I decided to take art classes that taught students the very essence of painting artwork. I had already been doing drawings since I was a kid, therefore the classes were easy for me.

After I completed the art classes I decided to move out of my moms and dads home to a apartment on the other side of town.

I first started doing paintings of average things like cartoon characters, the president, and celebrities which sold a little through my Facebook page, and some viewers would come to my apartment to buy paintings.

My family and friends started asking me to do personal paintings of them and their family. Other people would see those paintings, and come through for personal paintings as well. But the money I was making still wasn't sufficient to sustain all my bills by myself . . . .

One late night I was searching through my e-mails, one lady had e-mailed me asking if I could paint nude photos of her. Hell yeah, I thought to myself.

I e-mailed her saying yes, she e-mailed me right back asking the time, and place. I mentioned to her that it would be best if she could come over to my apartment the next night.

The next night came, and I awaited for her to come, she was a little late beyond our regularly scheduled time . . . .

I heard a knock at my door, I knew it was her because I wasn't expecting any other visitors. I looked through my peep hole, and seen this old lady standing there. Who is this old lady, this can't be the one requesting artwork of nudity, I thought to myself.

I opened the door she stuck her hand out to shake my hand, and said, "Hi, I'm Mary Ann I'm here to have the portrait painted of me." "My name is Steven, but you can just call me Steve, come on in," I said.

As she stepped in the door I begin checking this old lady out she was strap, she had a body better than most young women. She wore this beautiful full length black skirt with her cleavage showing with high heels on . . . .

She stepped in looking around admiring the artwork . . . .

"So where is the painting of the portrait going to take place," she asked when I became aware of her country accent. "Right here in the living room," I said. "Are we alone," she asked? "Of course," I said while looking directly in her beautiful blue eyes . . . .

She slowly undressed as if it was a strip tease, or as if we were getting ready to partake in the art of love making . . . .

I was stuck in a state of shock staring at this older lady beautiful body, as my cock got hard as concrete, I just wanted to give her vagina my cock in its entirety . . . .

"You must like what you see," she said. "I love what I see," I said . . . .

She laid down flat on her stomach with one of her finger slightly in her mouth, and told me this how she wanted me to paint the portrait . . . .

This old lady looked as if she was in her early forties, but looked wonderful, she was definitely someone I'd be interested in getting with . . . .

I started painting my first nude portrait as her, and I remained silent, it was as my cock refuse to get off hard, as I was on the verge of painting a masterpiece . . . .

Usually when I painted people it would be a problem, because people tend to move, she didn't move not one bit; which was strange that she could just lay there naked for hours . . . .

After the portrait was done I looked at it amazed and proud of myself . . . .

I told her it was finish she got up, and looked at it, and begin jumping up and down in joy. As her titties and butt cheeks jiggled as she jumped up, and down made my cock get even harder.

She paid me my money gave me a hug, and told me she will be back tomorrow to get her painting once it's totally dry . . . .

All night long I dreamed of that lady's naked body . . . .

The next day she came and got her portrait, and told me she'd come back soon for me to paint more portraits', I gave her my cell number so she wouldn't have to go through my e-mail or Facebook to get in touch with me . . . .

A week had went pass she called but I didn't recognize the number so I answered it, it was Mary Ann. She asked when could she come through to get more nude portraits done, I told her right now.

She came through, and I painted a portrait of her standing up naked . . . .

After that day she'd come every three days to get a nude portrait painting . . . .

I'm a human being, and heterosexual therefore I wanted to bang her more than you can imagine; but I didn't want to interrupt our business venture so I kept it professional . . . .

The fifth time she wanted me to paint a close up picture of just her vagina, I thought I was in heaven . . . .

After I finished painting her vagina she asked me to rub some baby oil on her. She laid flat on her stomach and told me to rub some baby oil on her back. As I begin rubbing it on her back she kept telling me to go down further once I got to the end of her back I told her I couldn't go down any further. She asked me why not I told her that I was at the end of her back. She asked me to rub some on her butt cheeks, I couldn't believe it. I started gently rubbing baby oil on her butt cheeks, my gently rubbing then turned to firm grips as she slightly moaned as if my cock was in her. I started to rub baby oil on her vagina as I gently slipped one, two, three, and then four fingers in and out of her, as she looked at me with the cutest sex face . . . .

I eagerly pulled my pants down hungry to give her my cock. Before I could stick it in she pleaded with me to give her my cock, and I did just that . . . .

When I first stuck my cock in her it felt wonderful it was tight, and moist it gripped my cock to perfection . . . .

I eagerly fed her vagina all of my cock as hard and fast as I could as she begged me to stop because it was too much pain for her to handle . . . .

Once I was done she begin sucking my cock without me even asking, and of course once she was done I returned the favor by eating her vagina . . . .

She spent a night over my house and we created pornography throughout the night on and off . . . .

Come to find out Mary Ann was fifty years old, and always wanted to show her body off to the the public, but never had the courage until I started painting those portraits of her.

After that night she placed my paintings of her in the nude on Facebook. Thanks to her my paintings sells were boosted. People from all over wanted me to do all sorts of paintings even those in the nude.

I never got the fame I wanted as an artist, as far as my paintings being in art galleries and shows. But I did get recognition from people that wanted personal paintings, and I made a lot of money off paintings . . . .

Maybe one day, possibly after I'm dead art galleries will exhibit my artwork.

As for me and Mary Ann she still comes over from time to time for me to do paintings of her in the nude, and for me to please her sexual lustful ways . . . .

Damn that was a bomb, Twon thought to his self as he begin looking for his bottle of lotion . . . .

CHAPTER 3

As time progressed along Twon became half use to and half tired of jail. The family and friends showed love, commissary, and visits every week . . . .

"What you doing man," Loco asked? "I'm getting ready for visits tomorrow," Twon said. "Aw yeah that's right visiting day is tomorrow," Loco said. "How in the hell did you get out your cell," Twon asked? "The police let me out to be the porter for tonight. I didn't wont shit I just stop by your cell to see what you was on, I'll let you finish shaving I'll see you tomorrow when the doors roll," Loco said. "A'ight," Twon said . . . .

Twon finished shaving, did a few push-ups, washed up in the sink, and went to sleep dreaming of the women he'd possibly see in the visiting room the next day . . . .

"Antwon Starks on that visit," the C/O said . . . .

Twon went to the visiting room, and to his surprise it was his pregnant ass girlfriend, she usually didn't come early in the morning . . . .

"What your pregnant ass doing coming up here to see me this early," Twon said. "I miss you," she said. "You just miss this big ass dick," Twon said. "Yeah I miss that to," she said. "I can't wait until you get out, it's just gone be me, you, and the baby," she said. "I aint even gone have time for you, I'm gone be with so many other ho's," Twon said. "Boy I wish you would. Why do you keep writing me them corny ass letters. How you gone be somebody daddy and you can't even spell grammar school words," she said as they both begin laughing . . . .

They stayed on visit for a while, both enjoyed seeing each other . . . .

After the visit Twon went back to the deck and couldn't stop smiling . . . .

"Damn nigga you smiling hard, tell me what you so happy for, so I can be happy like you," Loco said. "Nothing much, when the C/O's wasn't looking my girl showed me some things. I miss her," Twon said. "I know you do, don't worry big dick Bob will take care the pussy for you," Loco said, as they begin laughing. "She talking about my letters is corny as hell," Twon said. "Yeah, you gotta learn to be raw with the pen that's how you survive in jail, I'll read one of your letters later or the next time you write," Loco said. "Imma write her tonight when we lock up, if you be the porter tonight I want you to come through and read it," Twon said. "Okay I got you, I gotta go make some calls," Loco said. "Yeah gotta try to get one of these phones myself to make sure my visits get to rolling through today," Twon said . . . .

All the rest of the day Twon got a lot of visits. Loco got a couple visits as well . . . .

"Play time is over you cowards lock it up," the C/O said . . . .

"Fam you finished writing the letter yet," Loco said. "Naw not yet we only been locked up for about ten or fifteen minutes, come back later right before the police lock you up in the cell," Twon said. "Okay, ten, four," Loco said . . . .

"It's been almost two hours, you told me to come back before lock up time, we getting ready to lock up in a lil while, where the letter at," Loco asked? "Here it go," Twon said, as he handt him the letter . . . .

Loco begin reading the letter . . . .

In no time flat Loco begin to laugh out loud, and then handt him the letter back . . . .

"Man is you serious, you can't write no letters like this to no ho's, you can't write no letter like this to nobody. You gotta learn to write letters that's how niggas survive in jail. A gotta go the police calling me to lock up. I'll holla at you in the morning," Loco said. "A'ight love my nigga," Twon said. "Love nigga," Loco replied . . . .

The next morning and days to follow Loco tried teaching Twon how to properly write letters. Twon just didn't get it. Twon barely made it through grammar school, and only went to high school for three weeks before dropping out . . . .

PREVIOUSLY PUBLISHED
URBAN NOVEL

QUEEN OF QUEENS

CHAPTER 1

"Y ou sure this the right spot, man?" Slim asked.
"I'm positive this is the right spot. I wouldn't never bring you on no blank mission," Double J said.

With no hesitation, Double J kicked in the door and yelled, "Police! Lay the fuck down!"

Double J and Slim stormed into the crib with guns in hand, ready to fuck a nigga up if anybody made any false moves.

As they entered the crib, they immediately noticed two women sitting at the table. The women were getting ready to shake up some dope.

One of the women laid on the floor facedown, crying out, "Please, please don't shoot me."

She had seen many TV shows and movies in which the police kicked in doors and wrongfully thought an individual was strapped or reaching for a gun when they weren't, and the police hideously shot them, taking their lives from 'em.

The other woman tried to run and jump outta the window. Before she could do so, Double J tackled her down and handcuffed her.

Double J threw Slim a pair of handcuffs. "Handcuff her," Double J said.

As Slim began to handcuff the other chick, he began thinking, Where the fuck this nigga get some motherfucking handcuffs from?

The woman who was on the floor, crying, looked up and noticed that Slim wasn't the police.

"You niggas ain't no motherfucking police," she said.

Double J ran over and kicked her in the face, and busted her nose. "Bitch, shut the fuck up," Double J said.

She shut up, laid her head on the floor. As her head was filled with pain while tears ran down her face, with blood running from her nose, she silently prayed that this real-life nightmare would come to an end!

Simultaneously, Slim and Double J looked at the table filled with dope. Both Slim and Double J's mouths dropped. They'd never seen so much dope in their lives. Right in front of their eyes were one hundred grams of pure, uncut heroin.

Both women laid on the floor, scared to death. They'd never been so scared in their natural lives.

Double J went into the kitchen found some ziplock bags, came back and put the dope in them, and then stuffed the dope in the sleeves of his jacket 'cause it was too much dope to fit in his pockets.

"Man, we gotta hurry up. You know the neighbors probably heard us kick the door in," Slim said.

"The neighbors ain't heard shit 'cuz of all the fireworks going off. That's why I picked this time to run off in here, while the fireworks going off, so nobody won't hear us," Double J said.

"Shiit, they could've still heard us. The fireworks ain't going off inside the building," Slim said.

"Don't worry about it," Double J said.

"Lord, let's search the rooms before we leave. You know, if all this dope is here, it gotta be some guns or money in here somewhere," Double J said.

"Yep, Jo, I bet you it is," Slim said.

Double J walked over to the woman whose nose he busted, knelt, put a .357 to her ear, and clicked the hammer back. The woman heard the hammer click in her ear. She became so scared that she literally shit on herself.

"Bitch, I'ma ask you one time, where the rest of that shit at?" Double J asked in a deep hideous voice.

She began crying out and yelling, "It's in the closet, in the bottom of the dirty clothes hamper."

Double J went into the closet snatched all the clothes outta the hamper and found ten big bundles of money. He saw a book bag hanging in the closet, grabbed it, and loaded the money in it. Double J went back into the front room. Without second-guessing it, he shot both women in the back of their heads two times a piece.

Double J and Slim fled from the apartment building, got into their steamer, and smashed off. As Double J drove a few blocks away, Slim sat in the passenger side of the car, looking over at Double J, pissed off.

"Lord, why the fuck you shoot them hos?" Slim asked with hostility.

"Look at all the money and dope we got," Double J said.

"What that gotta do with it?" Slim asked.

"You know that that wasn't them hos shit. They was working for some nigga, and if that nigga ever found out we stuck him up for all that shit, he'd have a price on our heads. Now that the only people who knew about us taking that shit is dead, we don't gotta worry about that shit," Double J said.

Yeah, you right about that, Slim thought as he remained silent for a few seconds. "You just said something about dope and money. What money?" Slim asked.

"Look in the book bag," Double J said.

Slim unzipped the book bag, and it was as if he saw a million dollars. His mouth dropped, amazed by all the money that was in the book bag.

They hit the e-way and set fire to a lace joint as they began to think of all the things they'd be able to do with the money and dope.

Double J and Slim were two petty hustlers looking for this one big lick, and they finally got it. They had various hustles that consisted of robbing, car thieving, and selling a little dope. All their hustles revolved around King Phill. King Phill was a king of a branch of ViceLords, the Insane ViceLords (IVL). They'd rob, steal cars, and sell dope through King Phill, one way or the other.

Double J and Slim were basically King Phill's yes men. Whatever Phill would say or wanted them to do, they'd say yes to.

After forty-five minutes of driving, they parked the steamer on a deserted block where there were no houses, only a big empty park.

Double J began wiping off the inside of the car. Slim began to do the same.

"Make sure you wipe off everything real good. We don't wanna leave no fingerprints," Double J said.

"You ain't gotta tell me. The last thing I wanna do is get pinched for a pussy-ass stickup murder," Slim said.

Double J put the book bag on his back. They left the car, wiping off the inside and outside door handles, and they began walking to Double J's crib, which was about thirty minutes away.

"Lord, fire up one of them lace joints," Slim said.

"Here, you fire it up," Double J said as he passed the joint to Slim.

Slim instantly set fire to it. They walked swiftly to Double J's crib, continuously puffing on the lace joints. Once they made it halfway there, out of nowhere, Double J stopped in his tracks.

"What the fuck you stop for?" Slim asked.

"Lord, we gotta get rid of that car," Double J said.

"Why?" Slim asked.

"'Cuz like you said, we don't wanna get pinched for no stickup murder. If somebody seen that car leave the scene of the crime and they tell the police and the police find the car and dust it for fingerprints and find one fingerprint that matches one of ours, we booked. We'll be sitting on death row saying what we should've, would've, and could've done," Double J said.

"How we gone get rid of it?" Slim asked.

"Here, take my gun and bookbag and meet me at my crib. My girl there, she'll let you in," Double J said.

"You still didn't answer my question," Slim said.

"What's that?" Double J asked.

"How we gone get rid of the car?" Slim asked.

"Don't worry about it. I got it," Double J said.

"Let's get rid of it together," Slim said.

"Naw, man, we need to make sure the money and dope is safe, and we need to get these hot-ass guns off the streets," Double J said.

"Where is the dope?" Slim asked.

Double J reached into his sleeves, pulled out the dope, and handed it all to Slim as they departed and went their separate ways.

I hope this nigga don't get caught fucking around with that car, Slim thought.

Double J went back to the car, looking for something to use to set it on fire. He ended up finding some charcoal fluid in the trunk of the car, squeezed all the fluid out of the bottle all over the car, struck a match, and threw it on the car as it instantly began burning. Double J took off running. He ran halfway home and walked the other half.

Once Double J made it home, before he could even knock on the door or ring the doorbell, Slim opened the door. Double J rushed in nervously and slammed the door behind himself and frantically locked it.

"Nigga, what the fuck took you so long?" Slim asked.

"What took me so long? Shiiit, I ran halfway back, but anyway, I took care of the business. I burned the car up," Double J said.

"How much dough we got?" Double J asked.

"I don't know. I ain't even open the book bag up, I was waiting to you get here," Slim said.

"See that's why I fuck with you. Anybody else would've played me for some of the money and dope," Double J said.

"You my nigga. I wouldn't never try to get over on you. To keep it real, you didn't even have to take me on the lick with you," Slim said.

They went into the bathroom, locked the door, and began counting the money. Each bundle of money was a G.

"Damn, Lord, we got ten stacks and all this dope," Slim said.

"How we gone get rid of all this dope?" Double J asked.

"We gone sell it in grams," Slim said.

"Naw, man, we need to sell it in bags. We'll make more money selling it in bags. The only problem is where we gone sell it at. You know anywhere we try to open up at, they gone close us down," Double J said.

"We gone sell it in the hood," Slim said.

"Stop playing! You know damn well we dead in the hood. You know if we open up in the hood, they gone close us straight down," Double J said.

"We gone have to go through Phill," Slim said.

"Yeah, we'll get up with Phill tomorrow," Double J said.

"Man, don't tell nobody where we got the dope from."

"Nigga, do I look like a lame to you? What the fuck I look like, telling somebody about what we did," Slim said.

"I'm finna go to sleep. You might as well spend a night," Double J said.

"Yeah, I might as well spend a night," Slim said.

"I'll holla at you in the morning. I'm sleepy as hell," Double J said as he started to yawn.

Slim went and lay on the couch in the living room. Double J went into his bedroom, undressed down to his boxers and T-shirt, and got into bed with his wife, who he assumed was asleep. As Double J pulled the covers back, he noticed that his wife was in bed asshole-naked. I'm glad I married her, Double J thought while enjoying the view.

Slim and Double J stayed awake for a little while, thinking about the money they had and the profit they was going to make off the dope. As Double J closed his eyes to go to sleep, he felt his wife's hands gently slipping into his boxers, rubbing his dick.

"I thought you were asleep," Double J said.

"I ain't sleep. I was just lying here thinking about you," she said. She continued rubbing on his dick.

"Now you know you can't be rubbing on my dick without any lubrication. That shit don't feel good when you do it with dry hands," Double J said.

She got up and squeezed a little Jergens in the palm of her hand as he slipped his boxers off and lay back on the bed. She grabbed his dick firmly, began lathering it up with the lotion, and jagging him off at the same time.

As she thoroughly jagged him off, he pumped her hand until his nut unleashed on her titties, and she began rubbing the nut around on her titties as if it was baby oil or lotion. She then took his dick into her mouth, gobbling it and the lotion in all, swirling her tongue around it and sucking on it as if she was trying to suck some sweet nectar out of it.

Once it got rock hard, she began deep throating it, choking herself with his dick while rubbing on her own clitoris roughly while humming. In no time flat, he was releasing a load of nut down her throat. She stood, wiped her mouth, and slightly began growling. She then got on top of him and played with his dick for a few seconds until it got back hard.

She looked him in his eyes, as she grabbed his dick firmly and shoved it in her pussy, and began smiling. She began riding it slowly to get her pussy totally wet, while he grabbed her ass cheeks, guiding her movements.

Once her pussy got wet, he began slamming his dick in and out of her, enjoying the tightness of her moist pussy. She clawed his chest, moaning in the midst of pleasure and pain; she liked when it hurt.

It felt so good to him that every time he'd slam his dick up in her pussy, it felt like he was actually nutting.

As Double J began to nut, she was cumming simultaneously. As he began to slam his dick in and out her pussy rougher and harder, she began fucking him back. It was like a rodeo show as their orgasms exploded.

"Get up. Get on the bed so I can hit it from the back," Double J said.

She got on all fours on the bed. Double J got on his knees right behind her and began squeezing and rubbing her big brown pretty ass cheeks.

"Tell me you love me before you start fucking me," she said.

"I love your hot ass," he said. Double J then rammed his dick in her hot pussy, gripping her ass cheeks and slamming his dick in and out her pussy hard and fast while admiring the way her ass cheeks bounced. In no time, he was letting another nut explode in her pussy.

"Let me suck it," she said in a low seductive tone.

"Hold on, let me roll up a joint," Double J said.

"You know that I don't like the smell of lace joints. Why you got to lace your weed with cocaine? Why you can't smoke regular weed like everybody else?" she said.

Double J began smiling and looking her straight in the eyes. "Well, I'll smoke a regular joint just for you," Double J said. He rolled up a regular joint with only weed in it, set fire to it as she got on her knees with an aim to please.

As he inhaled and exhaled the potent weed smoke, she simultaneously sucked his dick, utilizing a suction method sucking mainly the tip thoroughly. The potent effect of the weed combined with her superb suction method and the moisture of her mouth felt so good that within seconds he released a glob of nut in her face.

He finished smoking his joint, and both of them lay on the bed. "You must really been wanting to fuck," Double J asked.

"I been thinking about you all day at work. I had to take off work because I creamed in my panties daydreaming about your dick going in and out my pussy and mouth. I been sitting in the house all day waiting on you," she said.

I done married a freak, Double J thought

They began to tell each other how much they loved each other and how their lives wouldn't be the same without each other, before both of them fell into a deep sleep.

The next morning, after Double J's wife had gone to work, Double J and Slim sat at the kitchen table eating breakfast, reminiscing about the stickup and the murders.

They glorified and celebrated the stickup and the murders as if they were professional athletes who just won a championship game or as if they had won the lottery.

It's sad how bloodshed make others glad. But this life some live in as thugs consist of no love. Other people were brought up to increase the peace and strive to earn college degrees, and live the American dream. But those who live the street life thrive on death and destruction. They rob, steal, and kill with no discretion, and glorify others' names who do the same.

"Hurry up and finish eating so we can go holla at Phill," Double J said.

"I'm already finished," Slim said.

"Well, empty the rest of that shit that's on the plate in the garbage and put that plate in the sink," Double J said.

Slim emptied the rest of the food in the garbage, put the plate in the sink, and went and grabbed the book bag.

"Naw, we gone leave the dope and shit here, unless you wanna take your half to your house," Double J said.

"It's cool, I'll leave it here," Slim said.

As they rode up the block in the hood where Phill was, they noticed many of the Insanes on Phill's security as usual.

Once they made it to where Phill was, Phill began smiling, 'cuz he was happy to see them. He needed them to take care of some business for him.

King Phill was a pretty boy. Stood about six feet five, half-Latino, half-black, with naturally curly black hair in his midtwenties. Those who didn't know Phill personally would've never believed that he was a king of a large street gang. King Phill looked like a pretty boy college student.

"Park the car. I need to holla at ya'll," Phill said.

They parked and got out to holla at him.

"I need ya'll to get some steamers for me," Phill said.

"We ain't on no car-thieving shit right now. We need your assistance on some other shit," Double J said.

"What ya'll need?" Phill asked.

"Let's step away from everybody. It's personal," Slim said.

As they stepped away from everybody else, Phill began trying to figure out what Double J and Slim wanted. Maybe they finna ask for some shit, Phill thought.

"Phill, we got some dope we need to get off," Double J said.

"What you talking about?" Phill asked.

"We need to pop it off in the hood," Slim said.

"What ya'll talking about, opening up a dope spot in the hood?" Phill asked.

"That's exactly what we're talking about," Slim said.

"You know ya'll can't work in the hood if ya'll ain't a five-star universal elite," Phill said.

"I told him," Double J said.

"Well, make us universal elites," Slim said.

Phill began laughing. "I don't just give out status like that. I ain't one of these phony-ass niggas that let people buy status. You gotta earn it fucking with me," Phill said.

Slim looked at Phill like he was crazy. "Earn it? All the shit we do for you and for the hood while them niggas you made universal elites be in the Bahamas some-motherfucking-where! We be doing all the shootings for the hood and all type of other shit for you and the hood," Slim said.

"Yeah, you do got a point, 'cuz ya'll do stand on nation business. This what I'm going to do for ya'll. I'ma let ya'll work in the hood under my name, but ya'll gotta pay," Phill said.

"How much we gotta pay?" Slim asked.

"That depends on how much dope ya'll got," Phill said.

"We got ten grams," Double J said. He was lying.

"Ten grams? That ain't shit. Ya'll work them ten grams for two or three weeks outta Argale park. In two or three weeks, ya'll should've at least doubled or tripled them ten grams. Once ya'll do, ya'll gotta give me a stack every week," Phill said.

Double J and Slim looked at each other smiling, knowing it was finna be on.

"A stack a week. We got you. We'll holla at you. I gotta go pick my girl up from work." Double J said. He was lying.

As Double J and Slim got into the car and rode off, listening to Al Green's "Love and Happiness." They were happier than a kid on Christmas Day.

CHAPTER 2

Three Days Later

"How much is that small black digital scale?" Double J asked the cashier.

"That one right there is a hundred dollars. But I'd recommend this white one right here if you're going to be weighing things over twenty-eight grams. A lot of customers usually buy that small black one, then later on down the line, the same customers come back and buy a bigger one, which is a waste of money to me," the woman cashier said.

"How much do the white one cost?" Slim asked.

"Two hundred," the cashier said.

"We'll take it," Slim said.

"Will that be it?" the cashier asked.

"Naw, we need five bottles of Dormin and a bundle of them little black baggies right there and two of them mac spoons," Slim said.

As other customers walked into the small record store, the cashier paused and began covering up the small area where contraband was being sold.

"Thomas, can you service the new customers?" the female cashier said to her coworker.

"Wait 'til these customers leave, then I'll give ya'll, ya'll items," the female cashier said to Double J and Slim.

"Ya'll sell scales, baggies, and all type of shit to everybody in the city, and now you wanna act like it's top secret," Slim said.

"Yeah, we do supply a lot of people with contraband, but those are only the people that come in here asking for it. We can't have contraband on display, because it's all types of people that come in here. A person might come in here with their kids. Or an off-duty police officer might come in here to buy some records. And if they see all this contraband on display, they'll report our ass to the city. We won't lose our store or anything like that, but we'll have to pay a healthy fine," the cashier said.

Within minutes, the other customers purchased their records and left the store.

"Your total will come out to three hundred seventy-five dollars," she said.

Slim paid her, and they left the store.

Once they made it to Double J's crib, they immediately weighed the dope for the first time.

"Damn, Lord, we got a hundred grams! I thought it'll be about fifty grams," Slim said.

"Yeah, me too," Double J said.

"Aw, we finna put up numbers if this shit is a bomb," Slim said.

"Showl is," Double J said.

"Why did you buy baggies instead of aluminum foil?" Double J asked.

"'Cuz we gone put the dope in the baggies. We don't need no aluminum foil," Slim said.

"But we need to put it in the aluminum foil so it can stay fresh," Double J said.

"Once we put it in the baggies then put some thick clear tape on the baggies, the dope will stay fresh," Slim said.

"We need to find us a connect on some quinine," Double J said.

"Naw, we ain't gone put no quinine or none of that other crazy shit on the dope. We either gone use dorms or sell it with no mix on it at all. We gone put three pills on each gram of dope," Slim said.

"How many grams we gone bag up the first time?" Double J asked.

"We gone bag up ten grams first and put it out there and see what it do. You know we can't bag up to much, 'cuz if it don't sell quick enough, it'll fall off," Slim said.

"That's my point exactly. That's why I ask," Double J said.

Double J weighed out ten grams on the scale. Then Double J and Slim opened up thirty dorms, which were actually capsules.

Double J and Slim then grabbed two playing cards apiece and began mixing the dope with the dorms.

"How many mac spoons we gone use?" Double J asked.

"We gone give up two macs for a sawbuck and see how that go first. If the dope is a bomb, we gone drop down to one mac spoon or a mac and a half. That all depends on how good the dope is. And if it's real good, we gone put more dorms in it," Slim said.

Double J and Slim grabbed a mac spoon apiece and began measuring the dope and putting it in the bags.

"I got some thick clear tape in my room, in the closet," Double J said.

"Wait 'til we get finished before you go get it," Slim said.

After about an hour and a half, they'd finally finished bagging up the dope.

"Let's count it up to see how much we bagged up," Double J said.

"We gone put twelve blows in a pack. Whoever sells the pack gets twenty dollars and turns us in a hundred," Slim said.

"How much we gone pay people to run the joint?" Double J asked.

"We ain't worried about that right now. We gone run the joint ourselves. Once it picks up, then we'll put people in play to run the joint. We'll worry about what we gone pay them when that time comes," Slim said.

As they sat at the table counting up the dope, Slim began to wonder who they were going get to work the packs.

"Shiiit, who we gone get to work the joint?" Slim asked.

"My lil cousins gone work the joint. They been sweating me for the last couple days about when we gone open up the joint so they can work. They juveniles, so if they catch a case, they mommas can just sign them out from the police station," Double J said.

Once they finished counting the dope up, it came out to twenty packs and seven odds. They bagged up $2,070, not including the two blows in each pack for the pack workers to get paid.

Slim began doing the mathematics in his head. "So if we got two stacks off ten grams, then we gone get at least twenty stacks off of the whole hundred grams," Slim said.

"Shiit, we gone get more than that if the dope is a bomb and if it can take more than three pills a gram," Double J said.

"Yep, showl is. Go grab the tape outta the closet," Slim said. When he came back with the tape, Slim examined it. "Yeah, Joe, this tape perfect," Slim said.

They put twelve bags on a strip of tape then put another strip of tape over the bags. They put the tape over the bags in order for the dope to stay fresh, and so none of the workers wouldn't dip into the bags.

Double J and Slim grabbed the dope and a .45 automatic and went to pick up Double J's cousins and set up shop in Argale Park. They posted up at the corners and in the park. One of Double J's cousins walked through the hood, telling all the dope fiends that they were passing out free dope in Argale Park. They dope fiends rushed to the park and spread the word. Two niggas who stood in the park, Double J's cousins, were passing out the samples to the dope fiends. A couple of hours later, the park was filled with dope fiends shopping for dope.

Double J and Slim couldn't believe how fast and how many dope fiends were coming to buy dope. Judging by the large amount of dope fiends who were coming to buy dope so soon, Double J and Slim knew they had some good dope.

"Damn, Lord, look how many dope fiends waiting in line to shop," Slim said.

"That's 'cuz the dope fiends that we gave samples to went and told everybody that we got good dope. Word of mouth travels," Double J said.

Within two days and one night, Double J and Slim sold the whole hundred grams.

"Lord, who we gone buy some more dope from?" Slim asked.

"That's a good question," Double J said.

As they continued to smoke and ride through the hood, they remained silent, trying to figure out who they'd start buying weight on the dope from.

"We gone have to start buying from Phill," Double J said.

"Phill got good dope, but it ain't a bomb," Slim said.

"How you know? You don't even use dope," Double J said.

"I can tell from the numbers his dope spots put up. His spots put up little numbers, but they ain't all that," Slim said.

"Who else we gone buy dope from? We gone have to get it from Phill," Double J said.

"Ride through Lexington and see if he out there," Slim said.

As they made it to Lexington, they saw Phill standing on the corner with a gang of niggas standing around him for his security.

"A Phill, check it out, Lord," Slim said.

Phill walked toward them smiling.

"Where's my money at?" Phill said.

"What money?" Slim asked.

"My g, what else? Money. I heard ya'll been tipping outta the park," Phill said.

"We'll get the money we owe you a little later on," Slim said.

"It ain't even been a whole week," Double J said.

"So what? I want my money ya'll been tipping," Phill said.

"A'ight we got you," Double J said.

"How much you'll sell us twenty-five grams of dope for?" Slim asked.

"Three thousand," Phill said.

"That's kinda high, ain't it?" Double J said.

"Naw, that's low. Anybody else I charge one fifty a gram. I'm only charging ya'll like one twenty-five a gram. At one twenty-five a gram, twenty-five grams suppose to come out to thirty-one twenty-five, but I just said an even three stacks. I ain't tripping over a hundred and twenty-five dollars. Look, right, I got shit I gotta do. Is ya'll gone need that twenty-five grams or not?" Phill asked.

"Yeah, we need it now," Double J said.

"I can't get it for ya'll right now, but I'll have somebody get it for ya'll later," Phill said.

"We gone have the g we owe you when you sell us the twenty-five grams, so we'll bring the whole four thousand with us," Slim said.

"I gotta go. I'll holla at ya'll later on," Phill said.

"Make sure we get them twenty-five grams today. Our joint is outta work," Slim said.

"I got ya'll. Don't worry about it," Phill said.

"A'ight, we'll holla at you," Slim said.

Later on that day, they were sitting in Double J's crib, chilling, when they got a call from Phill telling them that he was going to

211

send his guy John over with the twenty-five grams, and that they needed to make sure the four stacks was counted up right before they gave it to John.

Once John delivered the twenty-five grams, they went straight to Double J's kitchen table and started bagging up.

"How many pills we gone use?" Double J asked.

"We gone use three first, to see how the dope fiends like it with three in it," Slim said.

Both of them began opening up the seventy-five capsules and dumping the inside of the dorms on the table, on top of the twenty-five grams.

"Lord, if this dope is any good, we finna be getting money like never before. Fuck spending our money. We need to stack our shit and get into some real estate, then we can leave the dope game alone," Slim said.

"Yeah, I agree with you on that. You know all these other niggas be spending their shit, then when it comes time for bound money, they can't even bound out for ten or fifteen stacks," Double J said.

As they continued mixing up the dope, they both imagined of riches.

They next day, they put the dope on their joint, and to their surprise, the dope fiends loved it.

They finished that twenty-five grams in one day, and was right back at Phill's buying fifty grams this time. Phill was a player who liked to see niggas doing good getting money, so he sold them fifty grams for fifty-five hundred.

Once they put that fifty grams out, their they thought it would slow down some because the dope fiends would know from the last twenty-five grams that they ain't selling the same dope they had originally when they first opened up.

Double J and Slim sat back at the end of the park, admiring the view of the customers swarming to buy dope. It was as if every time the pack worker would bring out a new pack, the dope fiends would swarm on him like flies to shit.

"How the hell is our joint tipping like this with Phill's dope, and his joint ain't putting up numbers like ours?" Double J asked.

"That 'cuz Phill and a lot of these other niggas be putting that crazy shit on they dope. That's why I told you we ain't gone use nothing but dorms. Phill nam still checking a bag, but their turnover rate is slower," Slim said.

Within a month, Double J and Slim were the men. Their joint was putting up numbers. They bought new Cadillacs, new sports cars, and all. Their team of workers constantly grew. Hos coming from everywhere were trying to get with them. Throughout it all, they continued to buy dope from Phill.

CHAPTER 3

O ne hot sunny day, Double J was simply bending blocks in the hood, listening to Al Green, puffing on joints that weren't laced with cocaine when he saw her from the back in those jeans.

Damn, this ho thick as hell, Double J thought.

He pulled up to her. Once he saw her face, he became disappointed. Aw, this Cynthia dope fiend ass, he thought.

Cynthia immediately opened the passenger-side door and just jumped in his car.

"Take me to your spot to get some dope," she said.

"I got a few bags in my pocket," Double J said.

"What are you doing, riding around with dope in your pocket?" Cynthia asked.

"What else am I doing with dope in my pocket?" Double J said sarcastically.

"I didn't know you shoot dope," Cynthia said.

"Tell somebody, and I'll kill you," Double J said.

They drove to a quiet block on the outskirts of the hood, pulled over, and parked.

Double J gave Cynthia the dope to hook it up and put in the needle.

Once she hooked the dope up and put it in the needle, she tried handing the needle to Double J.

"Naw, you go ahead. Ladies first," Double J said.

With her right hand, she shot dope into the veins of her left arm. As her eyes rolled in the back of her head, her entire body felt as if it were taken to a whole other planet. Afterward, she passed the needle to Double J.

With his right hand, he shot dope into the veins of his left arm. As Barry White's song "I'm Never Gone Leave Your Love" played on the radio, Double J felt as if he was soaring above the clouds.

Afterward, Double J dropped Cynthia off at home and went and met Slim at his crib to shake up some dope.

"I bought a hundred grams instead of fifty," Slim said.

"That's cool," Double J said.

"Start busting the dorms down. I gotta go use the bathroom. My stomach fucked up from smoking all them lace joints," Slim said.

Slim came out the bathroom and saw Double J sitting at the table, nodding and scratching.

"Damn, nigga, you look like you done had a dope," Slim said.

"Naw, man, I'm just sleepy," Double J said.

So they both began busting the dorms down.

Double J kept scratching and nodding at the table.

This nigga fucking around with dope, Slim thought.

"Lord, tell the truth. Ain't you getting high?" Slim asked.

"Nigga, you know damn well I been getting high ever since you've known me," Double J said.

"Nigga, you know what I'm talking about. Is you fucking with dope?" Slim said.

Double J paused for a little while. "Yeah, I fuck around with the dope a little," Double J said.

"What made you turn into a dope fiend?" Slim asked.

"I use to be seeing how dope fiends look after they get high. Some of them looked like it's the best feeling in the world. Some of them be looking like they're walking on the clouds or some shit. Then I start to see how the dope fiends do whatever it takes to get money for dope. That made me want to try some even more, 'cuz I knew it had to be some good shit. Once I tried it, it felt like heaven on Earth. No lie, I'ma be a dope fiend forever. I'ma get high 'til I die," Double J said.

Slim looked at Double J with a smirk on his face, thinking, This nigga done lost his mind.

"Niggas always trying to belittle dope fiends, when they get high they motherfucking self off all types of shit. A drug addict is a drug addict. It don't matter if you smoke weed, lace weed, toot cocaine, toot dope, or shoot dope—you still a drug addict," Double J said.

"I can agree with you on that 'cuz I smoke more lace joints than some people use dope," Slim said.

"We gone have to start paying somebody to bag up this dope. This shit a headache," Slim said.

"Straight up," Double J said.

In the days that followed, Slim began to admire how suave Double J was as he was high off dope. As he walked, talked, drove, ate, smoked cigarettes, every way he maneuvered was super cool when he was drunk off dope.

Before long, Slim began asking Double J a gang of questions on how it felt to be high off dope.

"You steady asking me about how it feels to be high off dope. My best answer is you won't know how it feels until you try it," Double J said.

"I'm scared of needles," Slim said.

"You ain't gotta shot it. You can toot it. But it ain't nothing look shooting it. As that dope run up your veins, it's the best high you'll ever experience," Double J said.

Slim was still hesitant to try dope. He let his pride get in the way. He knew certain people looked down on dope fiends.

A couple of days later at a club, with these two lesbian chicks he dated and paid for sex, he began wanting to try some dope again. The lesbian chicks Tricey and Reese did it all besides dope. They snorted lines of cocaine, smoked lace joints and regular weed, and smoked leaf.

After downing a few drinks at the club. The girls sat at the table, snorting line after line of cocaine secretly, not in the public's eye.

"Damn, ya'll gone fuck around and OD," Slim said.

"That's only if you use dope. You ain't gonna find to many people OD'ing off cocaine, although you can OD off cocaine," Reese said.

"Have ya'll ever fucked around with dope before?" Slim asked.

"Hell naw, we ain't no motherfucking dope fiends," Tricey said.

"Shiiit, ya'll get high off everything else," Slim said.

"Everything besides dope," Tricey said.

"I heard that dope is the best high known to mankind," Slim said.

"Yeah, me too. But it takes control over your body. You gotta have it or your body won't be able to function right. And I heard the sickness is a motherfucker," Tricey said.

"I wanna snort a line or two to see how it feels," Slim said.

"So you wanna be a dope fiend?" Reese said sarcastically.

"Naw, I just wanna snort just one bag of dope to see how it feels. I want ya'll to snort it with me," Slim said.

"Hell naw," Reese said.

"Let's all three of us try it together," Slim said.

For almost an hour at the club, Slim tried convincing the girls to snort a bag of dope with him, and it worked. Slim pulled up to his dope spot.

"Tyrone, who working, Lord?" Slim asked.

"Ush working," Tyrone said.

"Why don't I see nobody shopping?" Slim asked.

"It's kinda slow right now, but you can best believe it'll be a gang of customers in line in no time," Tyrone said.

"Go get me three bags of dope, and hurry up, Lord," Slim said.

Tyrone rushed to go get three bags from Ush and brought it right back to the car. Slim took the dope and smashed off.

Slim parked a few blocks over from his joint. He tore open a bag of dope with his teeth and laid it on one of the girls' cigarette box. He tore a piece of the paper off his matchbox. He scooped up half the dope and snorted it like a pro. He sat the Newport box on the dash and leaned back in his seat to feel the total effect of the dope.

Within seconds, Slim had his door opened as he bent over, throwing up his guts.

If that shit gone have me throwing up like that, I don't even want none, Tricey thought.

After Slim finished throwing up, he snorted the other half of the dope off of the Newport box. He lay back in his seat and relaxed for minutes and began to feel the effect of being drunk off dope. The girls then snorted their bags.

As they lay there, high, they all thought within their own silent minds that dope was the best drug known to man.

Slim and both women wound up in a motel room. Slim's dick stayed on hard all the while. Slim had heard of the dope dick but didn't know that it was this intense.

For the entire week that followed, Slim snorted dope and smoked laced joints each day.

One morning as Slim went home, he got into it with his main girlfriend. She was tired of him spending nights out and cheating on her. She threw some hot coffee on him and swung at him a few times, leaving him with a few minor scars on his face. Slim stormed out the house and went to his joint.

Slim pulled on the joint, got two bags of dope, and pulled around the corner to blow them. He pulled back around to his joint sat on the hood of his car smoking a lace joint, thinking of all the good times, and the bad times he had, had with his girlfriend. He was still a little pissed off 'cuz she put her hands on him.

Double J pulled off, laughing.

"So I see you having problems with your girl," Double J said.

"How you know?" Slim asked.

"'Cuz I see you sitting there, faced all scratched up, looking crazy. I know you ain't let no nigga do it to you, because we'll be in war right now," Double J said.

Slim tossed the duck of the joint on the ground, bailed in with Double J, and Double J pulled off.

"Man this ho crazy. As soon as I walked through the door, she got to throwing shit, hollering, screaming, and swinging," Slim said.

"We all go through problems with women. That's been going on since the beginning of time," Double J said.

"Pull over for a minute. I need to take care of some business," Slim said.

Double J pulled over and put the car in park.

"What, you gotta piss or something?" Double J asked.

"Naw, I need to take care of something else," Slim said.

Slim pulled out his pack of cigarettes, then pulled out a bag of dope, opened it with his teeth, and poured it on the cigarette box. Double J remained silent. He couldn't believe what he was seeing. Slim then pulled out a small piece of a straw and snorted the entire bag of dope. Double J just sat there, looking at him like he was crazy.

Slim fired up a cigarette, looked at Double J, and asked, "Is my nose clean?"

"Yes, it's clean," Double J said.

"I can't believe you sat there and snorted a bag of dope after you been getting down on me after you found out I was getting high," Double J said.

"I been seeing how good you been looking when you high off dope. It be like you be walking on clouds or some shit, and I wanted that feeling. So I tried it, and I love it," Slim said.

"I told you it was a bomb, especially if you shoot it," Double J said.

Double J began smiling and pulled off, listening to Barry White's song "Ecstasy" as they drove to the mall.

Once they made it inside the mall, Slim became so happy at seeing all the hos there that he forgot all about what he and his girl had gone through earlier.

Slim wound up getting a gang of numbers from ho's.

When they entered this one shoe store, Slim couldn't take his eyes off this white chick. She was raw as hell. She was about five feet six, 140 pounds, a redhead, with black eyeliner around her hazel blue eyes, and red lipstick. She looked like a model or some shit. Slim decided to walk over and strike up a conversation with her.

Slim came to find out that her name was Angie. She lived on the north side of town. Twenty years of age with no boyfriend, no kids, or none of that. They exchanged numbers and went their separate ways.

All the rest of the day, Slim couldn't stop thinking of Angie. She just looked so good to him.

Slim went home that night and made up with his girl, and they got down from break-up to make-up sex.

Slim had never been with a white woman before but always wanted one. The next day, Slim wound up giving Angie a call. He thought she was gonna be on some phony shit, but he was wrong. She was real cool.

Slim and Angie starting hanging out together damn near every day. One of the things Slim liked about Angie was that she genuinely liked him for him. She wasn't like the other women that he'd fucked around with. They were only interested in money one way or the other. Angie wasn't.

Within a couple months, Slim left his main girl for Angie and moved in with her.

Within several months, Double J and Slim found their dope habits increasing. Having to spend more money to support their habits, for guns, for money on bonding their guys outta jail, and for having to pay more bills. This fortune and fame wasn't all what it seemed.

BOOKS OF POETRY
ALREADY PUBLISHED
BY ALAN HINES

JOYCE

1.Congratulations Mom

Congratulations mom u got your wings.
Don't worry about the kids and grandkids we good within reality
as it seems.
Gooo.....Mom gooo.....spread your wings go go up to Heaven,
meet the king of kings.
Spread your wings get away from all these no good Earthly things.
You finally got eternal peace reality not a dream.
No more worrying no more pains.
I love you mom but it's time to move on
to bigger and better things.
Go mom spread your wings glorify and sing.
You finally became one of God's angels mom you get your wings.
I see you in Heaven mom you look so pure
skin so clean wow God gave you
your youth back he turned you back nineteen.
Love you mom my queen of queens.

2.I Love You More

Mom I love you more and more although
now you rest in eternal peace.
Don't worry in Heaven your mom, brothers,
and my grandfather and family
and friends once again you shall meet.
Mockingbird lady let your soul fly,
fly away to finally be at peace. For the first
time in person Jesus Christ and his
father you shall meet. I must admit life without just aint gonna be
sweet. A genuine unconditional love always came from you to me.
Finally in Heaven finally at peace.
Mockingbird lady fly away and be free.

3.ATLEAST

Atleast you was always there.
Atleast I could count on you in times
of despair when no one else gave a care;
you was there when no love from others appeared.
Always had a place to call home, you gave keys
to the city, a major factor, a mayor.

4. YOUR ARE MISSED

Your are missed throughout the seconds each minute of the hours.
Lady of timely power.
Soul shall stand tall like a tower.
Memories shall never fade pleasant visions on
my mind shall remain devour.
Remember when you was a teenage nectar providing flower.
You're loved and missed throughout timely sessions each second
minute days of our lives with the 24 hours.

5. CHOICE

Freedom of speech.
Freedom of choice.
Love hearing your name through each
and every voice.....Joyce.....

6.NIGHTLY VISIONS

Nightly I vision you wearing a crown a queen.
On your back sits enormous fluffy white wings.
Lovely lady of dreams.

7. A Love Like No Other

A love like no other.
I was hers she was mines she was my mother.
There's no greater love than that from a mother.

8. LOVELY MOTHER

As my lovely mother lay down to sleep I
pray the Lord her soul to keep.
Even if I should die before I wake I pray the Lord
my soul to take.

9. HONOR

In the Bible it says honor thou mother
and father.
Mom although your gone I love even more regardless.
To your seeds your were marvelous.
Sometimes you used profanity to express problems
but you was always there through it all
and was always marvelous.

10. FULLNESS

And then came the stars the sunlight and the fullness of the moon.
Mom hopefully judgement day will appear
so youll be going home to
Heaven soon.

11. REJOICE

Rejoice for this lovely lady named Joyce.
After a bottle her opinion she'd voice;
made noise.
Lovely lady Joyce.
At Christmas time you made it rain
with the gifts and toys.
Extended love throughout the projects of
girls and boys.

12. CONTINIOUSLY FLOWING

Your first born love you to death shall
forever mourn.
Your family seeds still growing.
Legendary legacy of blossoming memories life through
us continously flowing.

13. JUST LIKE MAGIC

Magic.
Love that was satisfying.
Gratifying.
No denying,
Love that's everlasting.

14. THANK YOU

Thanks you for the life that was giving.
Love of life as a wonderful feeling.
A reflection of you through the creator as one
of your children.
Rest easy at peace in the eternal paradise
as a Heavenly citizen.

15. LOVE UNTO YOU

Love unto you.
Love and respect that's forever due unto you.
Memories that shall never fade anew.
Visions of you when you were young in your youth.
Days holding my hand walking me to grammer school.
Sweet melodies of a flute.
Lady sing to me the blues.
Wishing I could've been more of a better son to you.
A seed that grew.
My lady of love, love unto.

16. My Lovely Mother

Red roses on a pink and white casket of unforgettable love.
Only for you I'd shed blood.
To reach you I'd swim through infested waters of floods.
My lovely mother, my love.
As a kid at times I complain about the things we didn't have,
when I should've been grateful of what it was,
motherly love.

17. BEGOTTEN SON

Mom this is what it's become.
Your touch of gold, your magic wand.
Your begotten son.
A life built off the triumphs over struggles
of great aspects to come.
Without you I wouldn't exist,
or even have anything under the crescent moon slash sun.
On top I shall make myself a winner, I already won.
It's me mom, proud to be your begotten son.

18. Forever Exist

In my mind, body, soul you forever exist.
My childhood tooth fairy, my every year female Kris Kringle
that possessed the wish list.
My queen of queens my womenly prince.
You definitely will forever be missed forever exist.
Thanks for being a mother to the twins,
even through timely events.
Thanks for being a mother and a best
friend with most gracious bliss.
Thanks for everything, through me you forever exist.

19. Dear Lovely Mother

Lovely mother.
Never be another.
I love you like no other.
I promise to look over my younger sisters and brothers.
Shedded tears alone under covers.
Still working hard on manuscripts taking life further.
I can't believe your six feet under by dirt smoother.
A love like no other my lovely mother.

20. WHITE BIRDS

Lovely white birds fly from palms
of hands, fly, go far away.
Live to see another day.
In the skies with no limits forever stay.
Never perish away, even when it becomes the
darkness after the light of day.

Lovely birds don't let the other birds lead you astray,
fly, fly, far away go your seperate ways.
Lovely white birds fly far away.
Stay in the sky forever at your utmost high.
Spread your wings high as the sky.
Chirp lovely white birds, chirp in the morning as the sunrise,
light up the skies, chirp and forever fly,
to forever rise.
Lovely white birds fly.

BOOKS OF POETRY ALREADY PUBLISHED BY ALAN HINES

CONSTANT VISIONS

1. FREELY BE

Pay attention realize, and see what you see.
Allow hearts and minds to be free.
Keep it realistic, positively.
Let your brightness of light
shine to it's highest degree.
Love life and be free.

2. AFTER RAIN

At first it was the storming rain,
afterwards the sun, the rainbow, and pot of gold at the end showed
me happiness again.
Finally free, finally sane.
Love, life, loyalty, and being successful to me is everything.
At that's when contractual agreements, certifications,
degrees, and fater checks for hard work dedication exchanged.

After the rain that's when I seen the sun shine like
truthfulness of light it rays remain.
Revealed the hidden agendas, camouflage skin and
purposes of those I left in the past friendship could never
be never remain.

After the rain that's when I seen the greatness
and divine creativity of the world that exist in it's
entirety, atleast what's left, what still remains.....

After the rain.

3. SEE WHAT I SEE

See what I see.
Be where I've been.
Talk a walk in my shoes hurt your feelings
hurt your feet.
Burn like fire third degree.
Little kids with nothing to eat.
Daily gun fire like New Years Eve.
See what I see, as hearts bleed,
a land full of greed,
no oxygen to breathe.
See what I see from this cold
world souls go down under to lake
of eternal fire to never leave.....

4. Powers of Time

Time could never rewind.
If only we had the powers to turn
back the hands of time.
Give a sight, a vision to the blind,
leading the blind.
Live righteously, holy and divine.
Great things seek and find.
Get through troublesome times.
Prepare right now for in the future we shall overcome,
we shall shine.
In due time what was in the dark shall come to light shine,
we shall overcome we shall be considered divine.

5. WALKING TOGETHER

Walking in the winter wonderlands,
holding hands.
When boy meets girl woman meets man.
Yes we could, yes we can.
Each others biggest fan.
As if walking upon the clouds
while still on the soil of dry land.
A love that's grand.
Our love shall forever stand.

Walking in the winters wonderlands.

6. I'VE SEEN

I've seen those living breathing to those
in caskets dead.
Joy of happiness, days of stress upon head.
Seen those free, and those confined away,
calenders to shred.
Seen those that was rich, same ones poor, and mislead.
Seen those that was thought to be good but was snakes instead.
Seen my only love I ever had turned out to be a Lesbian in bed.

7. FROM HEAVEN

From Heaven rain down on me.
Let the father, the son, and the holy ghost
spirit watch over, guide me, bless me.
From Heaven rain down on me set me free.
Rain down on me, and let peace be multiplied
all throughout the streets.

8. CRUEL AND UNUSUAL PUNISHMENT

A time frame of cruel,
and unusual punishment stuck in a maze.
Running through time slightly conscious
as being dazed.
Permanent mental scars far from a phaze.
Reminiscing about the good
times back in the days.
This is life what was I thinking
that slight decision was made.
Did it to oneself got played.
Even when it's over institutionlize
memories shall be a repitition to appear
memories will never fade.

9. STAY PLEASANT

Stay pleasant.
Pray to go to Heaven.
Stop stressing, and appreciate
blessings.

10. LIKE

Like the coming of day.
Like little kids that joyfully play,
not innocently being struck by bullets of stray.
Like having nothing but good words to say.
Like the creator having things his way.
Like the seasons that roll around and change.
Like being happily married listening
to wedding bells ring.

11. WE WERE

We were suppose to be brothers of the same struggle.
My right hand would put no other above you.
But in your heart it wasn't true.
Confidential federal rat you.
Plots to kidnapp me robbery from strangers,
but set up by you.
We were suppose to be brothers, and I got love for
you but you heart aint true.

12. God Bless Thou Soul

God bless thou soul,
grow up, be grown, be golden, gold.
withstand the test of time,
stand firm in this world
that's so, so cold.

God bless thou soul.

13. Where Were You

Where were you when
commisary was called not even
a noodle in my box, no money to spend.
Where were you when I needed someone to talk to
an ear to lend.
I knew you when I thought I had a friend;
but where were you when I, when I needed a friend.

14. FELT

The traditonal love that had no end.
Vitilaity giving give in.
The love you gave felt like Heaven.

15. ABOVE THE CLOUDS

Be proud.
Keep your head up, and soar above clouds.
Do you be unique have your own style.
Love all the while.
Maintain keep your head above the clouds.

16. OF DIRECTION

Since of direction.
Love, affection, protection.
Sacret resting.
Love in confession.

17. LOVE EVERLASTING

I miss what we had,
what we share.
Loving was there.
Made me feel gigantic
king of kings of your layers.
Defined by consequences
of laws actions,
you still showed love,
moving forward no backtracking.
Memories everlasting.
Satisfaction.
Love Everlasting.

18. A PLACE CALLED HOME

A place called home.
A Black P. Stone.
On corners they club and roam.
Future unknown.
Slanging rocks and pockets full
of stones.
Names of slain soilders
still love on.
Carrying on.
Be Strong.
As older age hits reality comes along.
Boom I should've did right instead
of wrong.
I should've colleged and had
pension from job I worked long on.
I should've listen to those before me grown.
Know am old and grown,
living check to check living
at moms home.....
A place called home.

19. I GOT LOVE

I got love to give. Throughout the livilyhood of years.
Gonna take a lifetime gonna take years.
My dear I got love to give.
The love will get better in time throughout years.

Love to give throughout years.

20. MEMORABLE

Blessings called miracles.
It's gonna be a miracle.
Lovely and spiritual.
Memorable.

21. RUNNING OUT OF TIME.

Running out of time.
Police killing off mines,
and genecide we killing of our own kind.
O.D. off drugs can't stop the crying,
wish we could remain living instead of dying.
Blind leading blind.
High off drugs stuck on stupid stuck in time.
Losed love ones, losed my mind.
Running a marathon in mind,
running out of time.

22. SOMETHING WORTH STRIVING FOR

Something we all adore.
Something is worth striving for.
Something glameorous, galore.

23. Heavens Best

A chance a risk,
a livilyhood that wasn't filled with bliss.
Heaven must be better than this.
Funerals of babies,
and little kids.
Somebody just died again.
Losing real friends.
Heaven must be better than this.

24. PASSAGE WAY

I look down this dark tunnel see
a light to a passage way.
A passage way of better, brighter days.
A passage way of love that will be here to stay.
Sensational feelings all day everyday in such great way.

A passage where love was made, you see the upcoming
enchanting arrays of new days.
In loving memories that never fade.
And lovers that love being together spaces to invade;
in the light I seen through this passageway.

25. FADED MEMORIES

Fade away like faded memories.
I remember thee but the ungenuine
please don't remember me.
From non-sense let me be free.
I'm a vanish like a ghost in the wind
for to never see.
Faded memories.

26. APPRECIATE BLESSINGS

Once again life shall be our number
one most important blessing.
You gotta learn,
you gotta learn, you gotta learn from lessons.
Appreciate blessings.

27. BE

Let things be what they be.
Be observant, to see what you see, reality.
Allow inner spirits to be free from captivity.
Stand tall like the statue of liberty.
When it's said and done be who you be;
without trying to fit into false proximity.
Be, be free.

28. DESTINE

Destine.
Destine to be my destiny.
Harmonizing melodies.
A light that shined to a tunnel for me to see.
To see what it is for me to be.
Setting hearts and minds free from certain situations,
of anxiety to promise land to be free.
To forever trample off the falsehood but to let
realness for eyes to see.
Bring forth planted seeds by me for my future
blood lines to be able to achieve,
benefits able to reap.
It is destine, destine to be my destiny.

29. The One And Only

The one and only.
The one that would never leave me lonely.
The one that made his son out of a virgin,
as planted seed, forgiving for our sins we've freed.
My father whom are in Heaven;
the one that knows the real me.
Gave me this life to live from
my mother's stomach made me free.
The reason I'm able to hear,
touch, smell, breathe, taste, eyes to see.
To be me.
Gave my heart in mind to write poetry,
gave me a life to live, to be free.

30. Elevation

Elevate above and beyond so high.
Keep your head to the sky.
Live and let past ex-relationships die.
The righteous ones the creator has a plan
for you and I.
Be all you can be without no excuses why.
Elevate above and beyond with no limits,
so high.

BOOKS OF POETRY
ALREADY PUBLISHED
BY ALAN HINES

RED INK OF BLOOD

1. GOD'S REASON

God's reason for me breathing is to spread
wealth and goodness breeding.
Shine throughout the four seasons.
Give guidance in leading.
Sacrifice my life for others as nourishment for hunger feeding.
Tell the truth in which I believe in.
Be more interested in giving than receiving.
God's reason for me breathing is to give others life meaning.

2. TOMMY DREAMER

Dreamed of dreams.
Wanted to be king of kings.
Wanted to take away his own addiction of being a fiend.
Selling dreams, sold schemes.
Had women thinking they were queens.
Even in the midst of soap he wasn't clean.
Did his own thing.
Hustling people for a little change.
He dreamed of one day being on the movie screen,
the cover of magazines.
Wanted fans to scream his name.
Tommy Dreamer had big dreams.
But loved the dope as it seems.
Chase the dope like a fiend.
Would smoke crack and go into a world of dreams.
Felt periodic signs of a emperor,
ambassador or a king.
But in reality Tommy was a dopefiend with dreams.
Tommy Dreamer, dreamed.

3. That's a Low Down Dirty Shame

Majority of his life was wasted using heroic heroin,
and rocked cocaine.
Had no shame in his game.
He let it be what it was and did his thing.
Started off early serving in the game,
and even then came money and fame.
Eventually he wanted to try new things.
First started snorting just a little bit of cocaine,
and then graduated into a higher peddle, gold medal heroin,
and rocked cocaine.
In time his attitude and ways of living changed.
Things happen in the game, some I can't explain,
but his money became foreign and strange.
In due time he was a true fiend that told stories,
about ancient things, when he once had everything.
Right now today he's a addicted fiend, for it do anything.
Kids, and grandkids don't even know
him, don't even know his name.

Who am I to judge or call bad names,
but that's a low down dirty shame to forever be a drug fiend.

4. ABOUT

It's all about love and respect.
Those with guns, and will use them to protect.
Who shall really stand by your side under the threat of death.
In times of trials and errors who will accept calls of collect;
away from home show love, and respect,
not saying but actually doing
this and that.
Most gracious a traditional fest.
Love that will never ignore, and always respect.
Being true, flaws accept.....
It's all about love and respect.

5. HIGHEST DEGREE

Seasons greetings,
even when it wasn't the holiday seasons.
Loved my poetry readings.
In the bedroom wanted to be pleasing.
My child she wanted to be breeding.
My love forever she was seeking.
Told me all her secrets even things she did
with others under the sheets.
Genuinely she wanted our love to forever be.
She said I made her life complete.
She made it a treat everytime we'd meet.
She treated me like I wore the crown as she got
on her knees with an aim to please.
She made each day like the holiday season as
she loved me to the highest degree.

6. STAINED MIRROR

It was a stain in the mirror,
but yet and still she could see things clearer.
No Pilgrims or Happy Thanksgiving, but
instead roaches that fell from ceilings.
Gun shots of killings.
Abandon buiding living.
Mices that walked around as if they rented.
Kris Kringle ponded gifts on Christmas.
She'd bare witness to those that got high as the
only way to achieve a wonderful prism.
Over packed prisons of those that didn't listen,
didn't abide be the fundamental
written guidance of the literature.
She'd seen those before her that made wrong
decisions, she'd let that be a lesson
learned off others failed missions.
Those that's telling the ones secretly planted kisses.
Obituarys of those we love R.I.P. we miss them.
Lives that was confiscated over foolish and petty issues.
She blanked out and broke all mirrors, more
then seven years bad luck superstition
would definitely continue.
Took a piece of the broken mirror and slid both of her wrist tissue,
couldn't live the life of reality of a stain mirror.

7. Advance Planing

Advancements, and large numbered royalties I'm seeking.
Gotta leave my past behind,
the love of romance for the streets.
Twins, and N'dia my love is to keep;
thou shall always feed, already know what you need.
I'm a guide, teach, and lead, my love is always unto thee.

8. WRITING BOOKS

In chase and pursuit of a happiness
of success that's long over due.
Awaiting a dream come true.
Self made guru;
but I do what I do.
Manuscripts on top of manuscripts, some old some new.
Each day learning, earning currency due.
It's some hard work but I know success will
come to life through the truth,
once God feel like the time is due.....

9. PLEASURE OF PAIN

She enjoyed the pleasure of pain.
She loved playing sexual war games.
She loved yelling my name as she made me mad I forced it all the
way in her gave her everything;
she'd make me mad on purpose so she
could feel the pleasure of pain.
She'd love how in the bedroom I'd mistreat
her and call her the females dog name.

I honestly believe I treated her the same as
the rest that had went and came.
But to her our relationship was everything,
in the bedroom I made it rain.

11. MENTAL DISASTERS

Mental pics of my own self laying dead in a casket.
Killed by a teenager that had no father,
no parental guidance, he was a dirty bastard.

Mental pics of me being a slave,
and having to call another human being master,
what a disaster.

Menatal pics of me being in the midst of the dragon,
the beast empire doing sinful works being yelled at to do it faster.

Mental pics of me being stuck in a mental institution,
seeing illusions, confusion.

A prison of disaster, everlasting.

Souls that shall get eternal life in hell,
burn in eternal fire.
Drugs that took people higher.
A socialism of Pinocchio's liars and evilness of
preaching pastors.....
Mental images of disaster.

12. LADY LIGHT

Lady light what a sight of delight.
Craved to see you even in the darkest nights.
She brought things to the light, to life.
Kept it tight.
Did the things I liked.
Listened when I was right.
But remained silent as the poetry I write.
She said my poems should be recited over the open mic.
She said she loved making love in the bed each night.....
She shined so bright, lady light.

13. RUSH

They all told me, "slow down your in a rush enjoy your life you
work, and write books entirely to much."
I didn't listen because I wanted success to be lived up.
I wanted to be a boss that owned, possess lots of stuff.
While everyone else was at fiestas living it up,
I was either at work or at home writing poetry, music, and novels in
which I love, I lust.
I know dedication and hard work comes
those green and white papers
that say in God We Trust.
It was like an adrenline rush as direct
deposits had became grown ups.
I seen others that wanted but didn't own up.
I did positively in a rush so that check
to check living wouldn't even
come up, each new book would be a plus, and
success through me for we, for us
would come quick fast in a hurry, in a rush.

14. UNLIMITED EDITION

An edition of bodies that mysteriously came
up missing.
Poor kids that will never see Christmas.
Over packed prisons.
New crimes, and new laws being invented.
Those that's free with sick intentions.
Stressed out over bad decisions.
Ponds of drowning kids, dead bodies ate by vicious fishes.
Real life superstition.
Painful bodies filled with staples and stiches.
A real life unlimited edition in which we must live in
suspended until the creator officially says it's finish.

15. FACE REALITY

Face to face with reality.
Wars of casulties.
Segregated families.
A cheating spouses mentality.
Finding a decent salary.
Third worlds poverty.
A repeating of time of protesting against racism gallery.
And at the end of life we all must die tragicly.
Reality.

16. CLOCK

I'd sit and watch the clock wondering when
the madness and chaos would stop.
As the youth get killed by the flocks.
Shell shocked hearing gun shots that just wont stop.
Wishing I had the have nots.
Constantly being caught on tape, crooked cops.
Getting older with age as time repeats never stops.
Eventually my casket shall drop.
Father of time, clock never stops,
as I reminisce and continue to watch.

17. Dreams

Sometimes things are, sometimes things aint what they seem,
nothing comes to a dreamer but a dream;
guess who told me that, a dopefiend.
At that point in time I didn't understand what she'd mean.
She meant that a sleeper that dreams will
never live out their dreams to achieve
success and earn cream,
they got to get up spread wings, and breathe, and do things.
Eyes wide open, and seen, living out dreams.

18. Buying Time

Doctor's appointments,
exercising,
standing in health care lines.
As deaths are continiously inclined.
Leaving family members and friends behind.
Steady dying.
Never knowing who's next in line.
Never knowing when it's your time.
In reality we're living to dying.

19. LONGING

I want,and long for you.
Wanted to be right, not wrong for you.
I want to be with you.
Giving you a love that you could never come by or even close to.
I even wrote a song for you.
Our love will always be true.....
All along I long for you.

20. COURAGE

Courage and sight.
Power in life.
Worshipping God and his son Jesus Christ.
Will and might.
Studying and striving for better days and nights.
Not with a sword but with a pen winning all fights.

21. THANKS GOD

Thanks God for always be there before I
was even old enough to know you.
Thanks for being the only one there when rent is due.
Thanks God for at my older age making my feel brand new.
Thanks God for helping me live out my dreams
that hasn't yet totally came true;
thanks for giving me a pen, a paper to write
poetry to make the gray skies turn blue.
Thanks God for forever being true.
Thanks God for simply just being you.

22. TRAGIC LOST

A tragic lost.
From project windows infants and little kids was tossed;
by those whom hearts had turned frost.
From dealers, what their mom's loved was bought.
Souls were sold to the Devil for a low cost.
Street wars and murder cases were caught.
Some took it to trial, beyond a reasonable doubt,
they lost.
And the process continues from east, west,
north, south.....
Tragic lost.

23. No Substitution {Jean Hines}

She came with no substitution.
No New Years resolution,
her everything was to use the power of
prayer as her guide of movement.
She abided by each scripture Dueteronomy,
Psalms and Proverbs including.....
Everything I did she'd encourage me to strive for improvement.
She prayed that one day I'd graduate as a college student.
Her love was so wonderful, and so soothing.
She was against domestic violence, and child abusing.
Fifteen kids, loved God, an abortion clinic would never use it.
As time keep manuevoring could never find another her,
not even a substitution.....

24. WELL {JEAN HINES}

I knew that you meant well.
You sent money orders and prayed for those
that rotted in jail cells.
You told people to try harder after they failed.
The anointing of blessing oil, and the kingdom
of the Lord to come was the story you'd tell.
You loved all and wished them well.
Gave everything to church offerings in person
and through the mail.
Turned good out of the freshes things that had once went stale.
A sweet scent was your natural smell.
God Bless in Heaven you made it, you dwell.
I love you, and I wish you well.

25. LADY BLUES

This lady would sing the blues.
At a slow yet stylistic groove,
while being entertain by instrumental tools.
She'd speak her mind, felt as she had nothing to loose.
Pouring her heart out in the form of blues.
Sometimes that's all she'd do.
And I loved and adored her groove,
she was cool.
Dedicated to me she'd sing songs of blues telling me I love you.
And I loved her to.
A guru that song the blues.

26. GREATFUL OF BLESSINGS

Our father whom are in Heaven,
I appreciate your continuous blessings,
even the times when I was stressing,
you put me through that so I could learn valuable lessons.
Although I haven't been to church in a while I still try
to do righteous stepping.
No sins of sick sinful confessions.
To me your greater than any gift, jewel, or presents.....
The only Lord of Lords, King of Kings, the
almighty Heavenly Father of blessings.

27. STUCK

Stuck in a cave.
Trapped in a maze,
a permanent daze.
Overlays for the rotten under plays.
Painful memories that never fade.
Stuck, stuck in time, a cave, a phase, a worldwide maze.

28. A Pimp

I pimp my pen so it could write.
I pimp my pen so it could give the dead and the old a new life.
I pimp my pen so spectators could see
visions of sky rockets in flight,
as a sense of delight.
I pimp my pen so it could do the things I like.
I pimp my pen so it could go out and get me that money
throughout the days and weary nights, through amazon.com,
and other cites.
I pimped, I pimped my pen so it could write.

29. LOVE BEING

Love being dispursed.
Undid a bad spell, of a curse.
A caring for me sickness, as a nurse.
She loved me which was the truth,
felt good didn't hurt.
Genuine love that was always being dispured.....
Stray bullet hit her, had to bury her six feet under the dirt;
I wonder if she'd make it to the Heavens above the Earth.
Her love shall forever be dispursed.

30. REALITY CHECK

Reality came through like trying to cash a bad check.
Hot flashes and constant regrets,
problems can't forget.

Breaking necks,
popping tecs for respect.
Blacks gotta watch their backs for those that's assinged and paid
salaries to serve and protect.

Shell shocked street warrior vets.
Sexual predators that sweat.
No places of peace to rest within humanly flesh until death.

And when it's all said and done no one shall live forever,
one day we all must be laid to rest.....Reality check.

BOOKS OF POETRY ALREADY PUBLISHED BY ALAN HINES

THE BEAUTY OF LOVE

1. NATURAL HIGH

Lit.
Lit up the sky not like the first,
second, or third, but more like the fourth
day of July.
Believe she could fly.
Off life had a natural high.
Always wanted to be near
by my side.
Within her holy spirits
reside, demons could never
live to even get a chance to die.
Natural life, of natural high.

2. DISTANCE

Loving from a distance.
Relentless persistance.
Being away from home but still
love them, still miss them.
Far and wide love remains
coincide from a distance
amongst them.
Amongst schools of fish to swim.
Love that had light even
when the cold world became grim.
Love it was, love it is
amongst us, amongst them.

3. She'd Open My Eyes

She open my eyes to the sight of her rise.
I'd visualize family ties, moms apple pie, Heaven in the sky,
babies that will never even cry.
Legitimate reasoning why.
An angel descending on Earth in my eyes.
No surprise, flawless images of her
in my eyes.
No foolish pride.
No games being utilize.

She opened my eyes to love that seem to be cast
from the skies.
Gave me sight as I was once blind.
A love affair that I could never find.
Intellect of a female version of Albert Einstein.

She opened my eyes to what the creator had design;
what I was put on Earth to mastermind;
to be all I can be and shine until the end of time.

She opened my eyes to the true love in her
heart that was enshrined.

She opened my eyes to this love for her kind.

She opened my eyes.

4. ACROSS THE NATION

Beautiful as the the butterflies, birds, and flowers

across the nation.

Unity, loyalty, love,

that couldn't be replacing.

A floating star, an adjacent.

Lovely love across the the nation.

5. STAY

Stay with me as we grow old,
spend each day,
loving in a special way.
A product of the beauty love may.
The sun, the moon, the stars,
red Roses enchanting array.
Love me forever stay.

6. THE SUNRISE

The sunrise.
Blessing in disguise.
Blessed to see another day
opening eyes.
Finish line of a prize.
Upcoming features, uprise.
Angel in eyes.....
The sunrise.

7. LOVING FREE

See what I see.
Be who I be.
Loving her,
loving she.
Love that was free.

8. She Was Mines

Essence of time.
Making love to minds.
She was the greatest
love of all times.
She was a dream come true,
she was mines.

9. MERE PRESENCE

Mere presence.
Such a blessing.
To the youth conveyed
powerful messages.
Worshipped God daily,
less stressing.
Flourishing gifts,
presents.
Her mere presence,
was such a blessing.

10. Never Be Far Away

Never be far away.
Lovely one continously
shine my way.
Allow love to forever stay.
Together we love together we pray.
Love me forever and a day.

11. Minute, Second, Hour

Every minute, second, hour,
your love shines, your love devours.
Together we stand tall like tours.
You be the ruler of my
world love with each day 24 hours.
You be the meaning creativity,
beautiful as a flower.
You be my love of life
in every minute, second, hour.

12. Lovely Seed

A planted seed.
Love to breathe.
Goodness to breed.
The blossoming of lovely times
indeed, lovely seed.

13. NEST

A love nest.
A daily fest.
Say a prayer for those
in peace to rest.
Loving at it's best.
Bird chirp of love,
love nest.

14. WE

We.
We shall be dainty in
the breezing of time.
Spiritually inclined.
An everyday Valentines.
Love of a lifetime.

15. FOREVER MORE

Forever more.
Love you more.
For you I adore;
galore.
Love you forever more.

16. Forever Be

Shine for me.
Write sonnets of
poetry to rhyme for me.
Set my heart, mind, and soul free.
Shine for me, let our ove
together forever be.

17. LOVING DEEP

A love by the Oceans by
the Seas deep.
Love that only her and I could see.
love to be free.
Love we could feel even in
slumbers of sleep.
Love eye to eye things we would
see.
For I am you, you are me.

18. NEVER KNEW

I never knew in time that
she would make beautiful music
for my ears, and love to my mind.
I never that our love would stand
the test of time.
I never knew us being together
was God's will of his design.

19. WILL AND GRACE

Will and grace.
Love and taste.
Memories shall never be erased.
Love at it's finest,
through will, and grace.

20. LOVE TO REMAIN

Love to remain.
Happiness gained.
Substain.
My sweet thing;
sugar cane.
My livilyhood in it's
entirety, me everything.
Love that shall remain.

21. SATISFY YOU

I just wanna satisfy you.
Love no denying you.
Love unto.
Love that's true.
I just wanna satisfy you.

22. THEY DON'T KNOW

They don't know about this one whom enhances
blisses.
The tenderness of kisses.
Like a Mermaid that swim with fishes.

They don't know about my future Mrs.
A pleasurable vision of great premonitions.
Her and I will invade distances, conquer missions.
Ruler of existences.

The giver of love unforbidden.

They don't know about this woman and the world
we live in.

23. WHAT I LIKE ABOUT YOU

What it is I like about you,
you wash away falsehood through
the truth.
You treat others the way you want them to
treat you.
Although I'm old you make me feel brand new.
You bring the greatness of love that's due.....

24. PEACE AND TRANQUILITY

Peace and tranquility.
Loving rather free or
trap within captivity.
Loving without limits
of boundaries.
Loving that was liberty to be,
peaceful and tranquility.

25. THE BEAUTY OF LOVE

The beauty of love.
The beauty of joy.
The beauty of when man meets woman,
girl meets boy.
The beauty of love sessions,
the beauty love, happiness, and joy.

26. Love Beyond Life

Love beyond life.
Love as reaching paradise.
Love that seized possession
of happiness throughout
the days that turned to night.

27. WALK WITH ME

Walk with me.
Talk to me.
Share your secret thoughts with me.
Loving made easy and free.
Love me.
Stand by my side walk with me,
talk with me.
My love to be.

28. IN THE MORNING

In the morning when the sun
would come, that's when she'd
see light, me as a vision of delight.
A way for her to free her
lovely will, and might.
She was like love poetry flown to foreign
lands upon kites.
She was sky rockets in flight,
afternoon delight.
She was like a magician with a magical
wand to bring all good things to life.
After the sun came the rain and storm,
even dark nights, that's when even more she'd
love me with a great sense of appetite.

29. SHE SINCERLY LIKED

She likes his style, and wants him to plant childs.
She likes his image and value evading his space,
his kind couldn't be replace.
She likes all the things he'd say and do,
she likes him which was the truth.
She likes for him to play the flute and be the goverance
of his and her loving to.
She liked to do things for him that he wouldn't forget.
She liked to perform for him as no other men she'd
been with.
She really liked him more than any men that exist.
She liked him without her interest being condensed.

30. SHE GAVE

Vitality she gave.
Love she made.
Freedom as are ancient
brothers and sisters
when they were slaves.

BOOKS OF POETRY ALREADY PUBLISHED BY ALAN HINES

REFLECTIONS OF LOVE VOLUME 2

1. THE CITY OF ABUNDANT LIFE

She was from the city of Abundant Life.
Prayed to God through Jesus christ.
Sanctified is the way she chose to live life.
A virgin like Mary, Joseph's wife.
She made others take flight.
High off scriptures, and life.
Fun-loving, and nice.
For each one offering she gave twice.
Didn't care of others downfalls, or sick sinful delights;
she'd still preach to them about Christ.
She said once she die, she'd wanted to be buried
in the city of Abundant Life.

2. THANKS LORD

Thank you Lord for allowing me to wake up today to breathe.
To continue on with life, to proceed.

Thank you Lord for giving me a golden
heart that loves doing good
deeds.

Thank you Lord for giving me a paper
and pen to write poetry as a way
of being free.

Thank you Lord for the clothes on my back, the food that I eat;
thank you Lord for simply blessing me to be me.

3. EVER

It was said the love we had would remain
rather we're breathing or dead.
The only true love I ever had.
My happy days was converted over from the once tears I shed.
She'd convey to me her feelings out loud and
sometimes with a pen and pad.
Since the day we met no regrets, I'm glad.
She say she's pregnant, so now they start calling me dad.
A love that brought forth riches from rags.
The only true love I ever had.

4. LOVE BOAST

Not to brag or boast.
You the one I love the most.
An everyday champagne toast.
My ex-lovers are like ghost.
Keep you close;
a love I never want to let go.
You understand my style, my grind,
hustle and flow;
the love of poetry in which I wont let go.
It's so many reasons why I love you so.

Not to brag or boast but I truly
love you so.

5. TREE OF LIFE

Her love came like the tree of life.
Genuine natured, that of another time,
maybe I met her before in my former life.
The love of my life.
Her love was right I only wanted it once for the
rest of my life;
didn't want to break up and do it twice.
She faithfully served God,
and prayed to him each day as a latter day saint,
through Jesus Christ.

Her tree of life was right.
She kept her body, as a temple of righteous delight.
In life she wanted to do things that was right.
She loved me day and night.

In her back yard she had the apple tree of
red apples that was ripe.
It was nothing like the tree in which Eve,
Lucifer, and Adam brought sin to life.
It was the tree of knowledge, wisdom,
understanding, and love of life.....

The tree of life.

6. Finesse

In the most magnificent, beautiful, wonderfulest way she finesse.
Her love was better than the rest.
Her heart and mind she gave made me feel blessed.
Made me feel the firmness as an exercised chest.
Her love she gave it all and nothing less.
She'd never settle for less.
A way to be free from stress,
only her and I no contest, finesse.
I confess that I love the way she finesse,
better then the rest.

7. My Angels

They're my angels,
my Godly childs.
I love them all the time not only once in while.
The four together drives me wild.
Blessings as my kids, Godly childs.
I pray throughout life you'll over come tribulations and trials.
Allow God to be your guide all the while.
I'll be there through God later and now.
My angels, my Godly childs.

8. ANY GIVING SEASON

Any giving season her aim for pleasing was because
of I, me breathing.
Together never leaving.
From chaos fleeing.

Any giving seasons she stimulates my brain
by teasing knowledge feeding,
increasing speeding.

Any giving seasons she loved me for each and every reasons.

9. BABY N'DIA

I know you're only a baby,
and babies cry.
Sweetheart don't cry whip the tears from your weeping eyes.
Know that I love you, live for you,
for you I'd die.
That's one of the main reasons I write books of poetry,
erotica, urban so you can live down here on earth as it is in the sky.
Have a large piece of the pie.
A reflection of my truest love, and please
don't shed a tear even when I die.
A love for one of mines.
Baby N'dia you and I.

10. CELEBRATE, AND SING

Celebrate and sing.
Enjoy life in it's entirety, everything.
Appreciate life even the smallest simplest things.
Be your on light that gleam.
For knowledge fiend.
Be greatful for blessings,
celebrate and sing.

11. A LOVE

A love that was so much.
To hot for rumors, and the fakes to touch.
Much more, a plus.
Wonderful wonder woman that I met at work through an
appealing crush.
Oh how I love to kiss, and touch.
We on the same page, share the same dreams to fulfill
as a must.
I talked she'd listen, she'd talk I'd listen to her, together us.
No argurments or fuss.
Soulmates together as one, us.

12. SATISFIED WITH LOVE

She satisfied me with love.
Always peaceful no matches of grudge.
A love that flood.
Could even turn out clean things from stains of mud.
An angel from the Heavens above.
Her voice was like music to my ears because;
because she'd satisfy me with her love.

13. RIBBON

A ribbon that made me feel like I could fly.
Conquer any, and everything while living, alive.
One of my many reasons to live,
and I'm just not ready to die.
A ribbon in the sky.
A ribbon of love mutual together as a tie.
The realness I just couldn't deny.
A ribbon, a ribbon the Godly sky.

14. COINCIDENCE

It was more than a mere coincidence.
A love that was meant.
Time together well spent.
Growth of a woman, growth of a man.
Together we stand as lovers, and friends.
Hope we will grow old together until our life ends.
A blessed love that was no coincidence.
In the end came wedding vows, and pregnancy of twins.

15. Someone I Wanted To Know

Someone I wanted to get to know.
Feel, touch, and see how you flow.
Together, grow.
Continue to go.
I wanted to love her so.
Us together until we grow old.
From a distance I'd watch her,
and my eyes wouldn't let go.
I'd study her motions and distant ways,
and wanted I know.
Know in her head what goes on.
What knowledge she withold;
future plans, and goals.
I wanted to know if she was even interested in me
to get to know.

Someone I wanted to get to know,
and maybe share a love like no other I've
ever known or had before.

16. Remember Like This

Remember like this loyalty of a bliss.
Luscious lips to kiss.
Even when I'm not around remember like this.
The giving gift of love like St. Nick.
A princess, and be the prince.
Remember me and represent.
Together the precious time spent.
Whisper shoftly in my ear as love was meant.
Remember all the good times we shared,
the pleasurable moments spent.
Was there at my worst and my best.
Remember when for you I was much more than a lover or friend,
remember like this.

17. I HOPE

I hope that we can make it.
A love that was genuine no faking.
Rebuking of Satan.
I hope we make it happily congratulated.
A love that will be forbidden, forsaking.
Permanent stationed.
Always appreciated.
Glad, no regrets, didn't mistake it.
I want us to forever be together,
I hope we make it.

18. And Then

And then she converted her life over to Christianity,
never again in life would she sin.

And then she spread her love, and kindness to
the women, children, and men.

And then she treated me like an aspiration of love
that forever with held, suspend.

And then she'd chant softly to me day, and night
that she'd always love me with no end.

And then she became my first wife, gave birth
to my first son, the little brother of my twins.

And then the saga continues on, a love with no end.

And then.

19. Sunshine Within

You made sunshine come in.
Afraid to lose you I know another you I'll never find again.
She said before me she never laid up with another man.
She had long black curly hair, creamy
white skin adored by many men,
but she was even more beautiful within.
When I was only twenty something years old,
she, her made ma feel young again.
Even at 12:01 a.m. her light of sunshine would shine in.
When my spirits was down she'd lift me up,
when I needed a helping hand, she'd always be there a true friend.
She had a special ability to glow in any
and every room she came in.
Quite often she'd sit around reading nothing
but religious material in the Den.
I loved the way she shined to contend, my sushine within.

20. Sweet Like Candy

Sweet like candy.
Fine and dandy.
Polite and friendly.
Loving by the tons, plenty.
Never met alot of others like her,
not many.....
Sweet like candy.

21. Eye Appealing

Eye appealing.
Wonderful feelings, high as sealings.
Successful dealings.
Strived for a better living.
Life was for the giving.
Played Ms.Claus during Christmas for the children.
Put forth efforts to do great things through genuine feelings,
eye appealing.

22. TRUTH, REAL

She is the truth, and so real.
I love the way she makes me feel.
My lady hero, my wonderful woman of steel.
Provided massages, and medicine to cure my painful sickness of ill.
Would vividly express to me daily on how she feels.
Loving that was for real, and I definitely could feel.
On top of that she made her own money went half on the bills.
She never wanted to argue or debate she
just wanted love to be the deal,
and love it to feel.
The truth so real.

23. VALUED

Appreciated,
valued,
adored,
love I found you.
A dream that had came true.
A lovely lady a woman, a new.
My queen to be appreciate, and valued.

24. Garden of Love

Garden of love.
An angel from up above.
Warm hearted love that peacefully flowed,
a natural continious flood.
Fresh fruit of produce,
wholesome vegetable to share even with strangers
as if they were family of the same blood.
So filled with joy, peace, and love.
A dynamic duel of solutions to add more there of.
A back yard, a place to call home, a garden of sensational love.

25. LADY FIVE

Lady five kept the destiny of everlasting love alive.
Four she continiously opened up beautiful doors.
Three she allowed me to be free.
Two she let it do what it do.
One she earned it my love was won.

26. I Really Love You

I love in such a special way.
More than words can express or convey.
It seems as if I love your more each day.
Hoping you can forever stay.
Love simply seeing you walk my way.
You're hotter than a summer's day.
So special in a gloriest way.
I really love you and I'm here to stay.

27. Diamonds and Pearls

Diamonds and pearls.
A beautiful girl, a wonderful world.
A rainbow swirl.
Off springs of seeds fertile.
My lovely lady, my diamond my pearl.
To me she means the world.
A realistic love story that of another planet,
another time frame maybe of an addition world.
My diamond, my pearl.

28. LOVE DON'T STOP

She loves me, and I pray that her loving wont stop.
An enchanted castle doors locked.
King and queen of each others love, and others love not.
She loves me, let it be everlasting please don't stop.
Makes me feel love by the flocks,
a wonderful state of shock,
Love stay and don't stop.

29. IN EYES

In her eyes you could see the sunrise.
Living on Earth as it is in Heaven before the last
days of demise.
Happily ever after marriages, the beginning
of family ties.
Living forever no funerals to cry.
Her love was like a blessing from the creator
up and beyond the skies.
In her eyes I could see babies being born,
teaching the kids shoe laces to tie,
as they grow to teenagers teaching them how to drive.
She was and still such lovely lady seeing the burning love in
her eyes, dignity and pride.
What was hers was mines.
A love that was blessed, and cast from beyond the skies.
I could literally see Angels in her eyes.
This love of mines paradise in her eyes.

30. LOVE EVERLASTING

A love that came with no distractions.
A plus when it came to satisfaction.
Great hopes of being everlasting.
From palms of the hands of timely love let
descendants of angels be casting.
Nothing could interfere or come between
a love that was cut from a genuine cloth
of natured nutured fashion.....
Love everlasting.

BOOKS OF POETRY ALREADY PUBLISHED BY ALAN HINES

REFLECTIONS OF LOVE VOLUME 3

1. CLOSE MY EYES

I'd close my eyes and see a vision of her as if it was the sunrise.
Saint of Christ to be baptize.
I'd see her nuturing the masses of babies wiping tears from eyes,
whispering in their ears about upcoming tides, life as a blessing,
a prize to be all you could be in the road ahead that lies.

I'd close my eyes and see the happiness together her and I.
Us being together until parishing time, tides.
Love that shall forever reside.
When I was away from home she would pray for safe travels
on bumpy roads as I ride.
I'd dream of her and I forever together forever by each other's side.

I'd open my eyes to see her as a Mermaid,
an angel without camoflouge of disguise.

2. GREAT

Estate, peaceful from madness a route of escape.
That of another time, another date.
To share to spread love anxious anticipated can't wait.
Down the right path kept straight.
An estate, making of faith which was great,
broke bread ate off the same plate,
lovely as the Carribean on a summes's day.
Lovely, wonderful, and great.

3. AN ARRAY

An array of flowers, bouquet.
The shining the light the sun rays.
The birth of child on any giving day.
Joyfully as worry free kids play.
Never going astray.
Musicians pleasant music continue to play.
Let your love, your light shine, shine my way.

4. SHE, HER, I, WE

She, her, I, we forever together as one to be.
Coast through the days of life to ever be free.
She made me feel the realist joy of what love was, is, should be.

5. BLESSING I GOT

Pleasant, delightful, soothing feeling like a cash crop.
Love I never wanted to stop.
Each day I pray, grateful for the blessing I received I got.

6. DEEP AFFECTION

Deep affection.
Love, protection.
Blessing.
Tender caressing.
My dearest presents.
I adore, mi amor, my deepest affection,
lovely, a blessing.

7. Took My High

She took me high.
High to the sky.
To fly, to get by,
love that will never get old to die.
She was the reason why love came flowing from the sky.
Still in all living to die.
But she kept the hope opportunity
of living alive taught the world
to sing in perfect harmony, and taught me how to
fly.

8. She Gave Me

She gave me her love, she gave me her mind.
She gave her vitality, she gave her time.
Beautiful was her heart and mind.
Was that of past history, ancient times,
and the future combine.
She gave me her knowledge,
and soul throughout time.
She gave me her love she gave me her mind.

9. MAKE IT

Make it whenever, however.
Make it last forever together.
Make it however, whenever, together,
loves going last forever.

10. WISH YOU WELL

I wish you well.
Your name rings bell.
Love letters flown like kites to
those trapped in cells.
Although were currently apart,
I stilll wish you well,
you deserve to be in white, wedding veil.
For you I throw coins in a wishing well.
I love you, I miss you, and I wish you well.

11. FOREVER WE SHALL

Forever we shall love.
Forever we shall be together because of
the man above.
Forever we shall be as one,
one love.

12. MORE

More than a name.
Fortune and fame.
Love in abundance came.
My Everything.

13. She Was A Blessing

She was a blessing.
I'm confessing.
Lovely as a new born laid
in a basket.
A blessing.

14. LOVELY AS

Lovely as can be.
Lovely and free.
Lovely as summers eve.
Lovely as can be.

15. SHE WAS MORE

She was more like my great heights.
A beautiful sight.
A great sense of delight.
Love of the day,
love of the night,
love of my life.

16. The Stars The Moon

The stars the moon.
Those away from home,
will be coming home soon.
Days of gloom.
The sunlight, moonlight,
stars and the moon.

17. Look Into My Eyes

Look into my eyes and you'll
see that my heart is yours as a prize.
Look into only my eyes as I'll hypnotize.
Look into my eyes for you'll see no cries;
look into my eyes and the rest of our lives,
our love will never take a dive.

18. You Gotta Smile

You gotta smile that wakes up the dead.
You gotta smile that makes no tears to be shed.
You gotta smile that has more wheat and nutrition
than bread.
You gotta smile that makes Lucifer'd sins shred.

19. LOVING

Loving at it's best.
Loving better than the rest.
Loving as a daily fest.

20. Sweet Lady Be

Sweet lady be mines.
Sweet lady be my everyday Valentines.
Sweet lady be my daily shine.

21. Loving Without

Loving without regret.
Love without a reject.
Loving in which didn't break
a sweat.

22. THE SAPRKLE

The sparkle in her eyes
you could see the sunrise.

The sparkle made me feel
uplifting on the rise.

The sparkle you could see
it in her eyes.

23. A Great Uprise

A great uprise.
Love enterprise.
Angel in eyes.

24. THE LOVE OF LIFE

The love of life.
Double the pleasure,
twice as nice.
Garden of Eden, paradise.

25. Be My Shine

Be my shine.
Be my peace of mind.
Be my love of a lifetime.

26. Loving Instead

Loving instead.
Loving as the best calcium to be fed.
Loving as together we break bread.

27. Daylight Savings

Daylight savings.
Love so amazing.
Beautiful black raven.

28. EMPIRE

Empire.
My female sire.
The kingdom on Earth,
king and queen with no retire.
My love, my empire.

29. Lovely One

Loveliest one.
Beautifulist one.
Wonderful one.
Lovely and fun.
Lovely one.

30. YOU AND ME

You and me.
Her, I, and she.
Loving free.

BOOKS OF POETRY ALREADY PUBLISHED BY ALAN HINES

TRUE LOVE POETRY

1. FREE LOVE

The same air we breathe.
Together happiness acheived.
A special lady, a special part of me.
Love for us to see.
I love her she loved me whole-heartidely.
Love that was free.

2. LOVELY, AND COURAGIOUS.

Sensational,
motivational,
all the time not occasions.

Couragious.
Love contigious.
Abnormal, love in abudance outragious.
A performer of stages.
A memory of love that could never be faded.

3. CHERISHING CRUSH

For her I had a cherishing crush,
A fondness I loved so much.
When apart I couldn't wait to get together to kiss, hug,
hold hands the gentle touch.
There was no one as her, or just I we was together as one us.
An enchanting overwhelming crush.
Us forever together is a must.
I adore you so much my sweet lady,
my cherishing crush.

4. THROWN

In the comfort of our love zone.
A special designated place we called home.
Would never leave you alone.
Study ways to make you feel like a queen of a thrown.
For you wrote poetry, sent you text messages of love,
each time you were away from home.
Knew and appreciated the woman you've came to be,
oh how you've grown.
An all star of comfort, of love, of a pleasurable tone,
a love I could call my own, a love for my queen of the thrown.

5. PARTIPATED

Participated.
Congratualted.
Under rated, before her time out dated.
Finally made it.
Struggled and strived to be successful
through hard work dedication and patience.
Participated.

6.SIMPLY MEANT

Simply marvelous.
Like a special event.
Time well spent.
Heavenly, Heaven sent.
Fresh like mints.
A natural perfume scent.
Simply adorable, you and I were meant.

7. ARRAY OF SUMMER

The enchanting array of summer.
Someday I'd make you my spouse, and a mother.
To me you are an excellent lover.
A friend that always encourages me to go futher.
Your mom and dad made a lovely daughter.
Your dreams I promise to be more supportive.
Guidance and order.
The enchanting array of summer, summer's daughter.

8. HURRY

Some say you shouldn't rush it,
but her love came in a hurry.
She seemed to be stress free, never worried;
she put everything in God's hands that was her true story.
She didn't date to much, didn't have any
kids wasn't interested in watching
Maury.
She was genuine she let love come in a hurry.
Kept her mind and body clean wasn't poisioned or dirty.
Stayed in library of books to be an impending professor
she was worthy.
She was there in my time of need lovely lady, lovely flurry.
Her love came fast in a hurry.

9. Complete Me

Complete me.
Freed me.
Would travel across the globe to see me.
Wanted always be near me.
Together is where she wanted us to always be.
My lady of liberty.
My lady Mermaid of the sea.
The one completed, please never leave.

10. POWERED LIVES

Empowered lives.
Kept the youthfulness, and desire of love, and hope alive.
An inspirational pride.
Within her chaos, and confusion and been died.
Side by side, as loyalty and affection coincide.
Continued to step, and stride.
The excitement even stayed alive.
Touched the heart and mind of others by empowering lives.

11. REFRESHING DELIGHT

A refreshing delight.
An Earthly paradise.
A straight path, the ways of being right.
The love of life.
Sunny days that came even after the darkest nights.
Refreshing delights.

12. A Wonderful Feeling

Oh, what a wonderful feeling.
The love that was being giving, fufilling.
Home, always live, living.
Pleasure was all mines, a privilege.
Always able, and willing.
The loveliest love, my queen of hearts
of dealings.

Oh, what a wonderful feeling love that
was being received, and giving.

13. TREND SETTER

Enjoyed my poetry, and love letters.
A trend setter.
Second time around she always tried to make things better.
She'd provide shelter for the homeless so they wouldn't be stuck
out in the bad weather.
Cut from the same cloth, birds of a feather that flocked together.
Whatever I decided she was down for whatever.
She'd dream of freedom like the late great husband of Coretta.
She'd read my poetry out loud, but secretly read my love letters.
She told me to keep writing, and things would get better.
She was fashionable, a designer, people followed her trend,
trend setter.

14. I WISH

I wish....
I wish to spend, savour each moment together
as a bliss.
Luscious lips to kiss.
Swim through seas like schools of fish.

I wish you could be an adult that made Santa Clause
gift list.

A queen for a king, a princess for a prince.

I wish we could live a life alone without a plot
or twist in a world as we're the only two that exist.

I wish....

15. THAT GIRL

That girl has my heart plus mind.
I love more each time.
Symbolic signs.
A queen of hearts, divine.
The best of times.
Her and I as one combined.
That girl is so fine proud to have her mines.

16. Life's Entirety

Her life in it's entirety, shall gave me it's all.
She'd stand me back up after a fall, letting me know
you must walk but only after you crawl.
Loved me throughout my exterior flaws.
She'd go against the Judicial system if I
decided to break the court systems
laws.
She gave my love, and devoted her life with no pause.
She gave me everything in it's entirety,
she gave me her all.

17. SPECIAL KIND

Never misunderstood.
Stimulates, stocks of woods.
Created atmospheres, all good.
Wishing our love to forever remain, wish it would.
Special kind, special kind of love as it took a stand,
stood.

18. STANDS

Stand for something or fall for anything.

Stand on your own two feet, legally an
adult at the age of eighteen,

Stand back up even after you fall, as it seems,
women and men, kings and queens.

19. WHEN LOVE CAME

When love came.
An intoduction, love at first sight
a mutual feeling of being the same.
Kept me sane, able to maintain.
A stimulator, a peace maker, through brains.
I definitely could gain.
Fortunate and fame.
A love that was righteous, no loop holes
or anything.
My everything.
My princess, my queen.....
She even wanted to have my last name.
When love came.

20. BELIEVE ACHIEVE

You gotta believe that greatness you
can and will achieve.
Success is a must indeed.
Spouses should, must be appreciated,
and please.
Fathers provide, feed.
Unlock all the positively, with positive keys.
Believe, achieve.

21. Never Let Go

It's hard for me to let go.
My body is still calling for you,
my heart is yearning for the tenderness of your soul.
We've been seperated for years but I miss you, and love you so.
For you my love continues grow.
For you my heart, and mind just wont let go.
For you I pray that God blesss you soul.
For you my love, my love shall never let go.
For you the attachment within my heart shall never let go.
I love you so.

22. SWEET BABY(N'DIA)

Sweet little baby.
I love you like crazy.
Years from now I see you as a
college student a productive
young lady with a purpose, a duty,
daily.
Things I'll never imagine you'll
make it happen without the probability
of maybe.....
Sweet baby.

23. HONORABLE MENTION

Honorable mention.
We talk alot, pay close attention,
all things I had to say she'd vividly listen.
From a distance blowing kisses.
Planned on way day being the misses.
Been together with no hiding intention.
Peacefully swin through the Seas like schools
of fishes without sharks or other viscious fishes
in existence.
No matter how far we went in the love of life,
she felt like her appreciation for me was never
finished.
It seemed as we've met before, but this time
it's more fulfilling, replinished.
She was miss independent, had a 401k plan,
and after many years of working she'd retire
to a pention.
A love affair always honor, and mention.
She was honorable, an honorable mention.

My truest love.
My truest love cast from
Heavens above.
Love it is, love it was.
Love as an art, sport,
love in it's fullest,
the truest of love.

25. The Highest of Ground

The highest of ground.
Love that runs around and around.
Love that forever mound.
Love that reached the skies
from the bottom, from the ground.

26. FROM NEAR OR FAR

From near or far,
I love who you are.
A superstar, a shining star.
The greatest love thus far.
Love from near or far.

27. MUSICIAN/PEDIATRICIAN

She was a Musician witha doctors degree
as a Pediatrician.
People of all walks of the world would hear
her music stop what they was doing to listen.
She had a variety of music that made people
see visions; Rock and Roll, Country Western, and
Rap lyrics that had premonitions.
Her music was soothing and had people
making wise decisions.
As all good times were being blended.

A pediatrician that had babies on
health care grow up plans with good
intentions.....

She was a Musician, and Pediatrician.

28. LOVE AROUND

Love around the clock.
Loving my daily stock.
Love I wanted non stop.

29. Love Came Quick

Love came quick, and in a hurry.
Stress free without worries.

Love came quick in a hurry,
lovely birds chirping freely flying
without worries.

Love came quick in a hurry
no blurred visions, no flurry.

Love came quick in a hurry.

30. Love All The Time

Love all the time.
Love to my mind.
Love of the best kind.

BOOKS OF POETRY ALREADY PUBLISHED BY ALAN HINES

LOVE VOLUME 1

1. ON TOP

On top loving non stop
around the clock.
A system of loving that rocked.

On top we'd watch the sunrise
making plans for the new days that shall flock.

On top they'll be love non stop.

2. IN CHRIST

In Christ things will become.
Became unified as one.
Divided eternal life and death
forgiving for sins God's son.
Love shall become the tree
of love to become.
All things in the dark shall shine
like the light of Christ,
believe in him and it shall become.

3. Part Of My Identity

Part of my identity.
Spiritually.
Religiously.
Liberty.
Always have a place in my
heart part of me, part of my identity.

4. THANKS FOR BLESSINGS

Thank God for his many blessings.
Love of life less stressing.
Thank God for living life still living
in each timely session.

5. REACHED

Reached sought and seeked.
Love that stood through the distance
reached.
From head to feet reached.
Sweet like the nectar from strawberry or peach.
Love was made famous would be wherever I was at reached.

6. Better Images

Better images crossing lines
of schrimage pacing as a turtle
to the line of finish.
Love that had no ending.
Constant visions of her,
the best images.

7. SEVEN

Her parents named her seven,
because of one through seven she was a blessing.
Two because she was wonderful a guru.
Three because she gave them a sense of hope,
a way to let love,
and life be free.
Four because she'd bring forth life which was beautiful,
and they wanted to give birth to more.
Five is because she had a vibrant vibe that
kept hope alive.
Six was because she kept them wanting
better lives in the mix.
They named her seven because she was
a blessing from Heaven.

8. AT LAST

At last love came to pass.
The unveiling of a veil, a mask.
Loves gonna last.
Came like a sudden shocking blast.
At last love came to pass.

9. SEEDS THAT GREW

Who'd ever knew from a simple planted
seed something beautiful and new grew.
Memorable melodies from a flute.
The intellect of study groups.
Love and respect that was always there and due,
and was true.
She was colorful, wonderful, beautiful, and all brand new.
A seed that grew.

10. I Wish I Had

I wish I had someone like me.
Someone that peacefully roam the streets.
A poet like me that write poetry.
Someone that cries out,
and pray for those locked
behind bars to be free.
Interesting in hunger to feed,
helping those in need.
Instead of poverty, thinking positively.
Giving visions, tools of life, keys.
Someone that's heart, and mind is free.
I wish I had that special lady to be;
someone who is just like me.

11. Dream or Reality

Dream or reality.
Pleasurable formality.
Let's build, let's build
a family.
Turn a dream into reality.

12. FIRST SIGHT

Love at first sight,
her beauty was brighter than the sun.
Love and happiness shall soon
combine as one.
Peace sits as destiny to become.
Birth of my seed, first son.
Love at first sight beautiful
the rising the sun, fireworks in the air stun.
Beautiful as a new born to become.

13. ORDAIN

Knowlegde in ears to inherit ordain.
The best lady of all times, a great dame.
My love of life in which she came.
My honey, my sweetheart, my sugar cane.

14. MERE

Her mere presence is a blessing.
Cherishing.
Treasuring.
Caring.
Lovely and daring.

15. FOR WE

For we shall be together until the end of time.
For we shall be together love undying.
For we shall be together as the love of yours
the love of mines.

16. CONSTANTLY

Constantly, I'd love she.
Constantly, daily I'd think of thee.
Constantly, she was my return from love I gave
previously.
Constantly and always she was my love to be.

17. NOT ALONE

I can't do it alone although I'm grown
I feel like an infant on my own.
Hearing impaired over the phone.
I need you home.
With me is where you belong.
No seperation zones.
Divorce attorney leave me alone.
My life, my wife, please come back home.

18. MY LIFE

My life she is and was.
My love, my life my worlds is yours.
Free flow of love just for you but global
upon tours.
My Life, my love is for you, yours.

19. MARY

God thank you for giving unto Mary Jesus.
I write poetry of course but in reality I could
never express the greatness of your everlasting
love succeeded.
Love as giving birth the air we breathing.
I shall worship no other God for any giving reason.
The God I worship sacrificed the life of his
only begotten son for our sins blood shed, bleeding.

20. LOVELY AS

Lovely as the leaves that fall in Autumn.

Lovely as the growth of planted seeds.

Lovely as it is being free.

Lovely as can be.

21. Love All the Time

Love all the time.
Love together as we shine.
Love having you as mines.
Love making love to your mind.
Love you, you're intelligent, divine.
Love you more each time.

22. SENSATIONAL TWIST

An sensational twist.
A love like no other,
never knew a love like this.
A kiss like the french.
A peaceful whistle that makes
love and life to be meant.

23. CONTINUE TO PRAY

Continue to pray.
Love shall forever shine my way.
Love poerty to convey.

24. DIFFERENT

She was different and special to be.
Cool like the summer breeze, the wrongfully
convicted to be free.
She was love to me.
She was the greatest she could be.
She was different, special, lovely, spirit of being free.

25. KEPT ME

Kept me up, up on my feet.
Uplifted me.
Gave me knowledge food for my soul
to feed.
Constant visions of her to see.
She kept me up,
she kept me on my feet.

26. GODDESS

She was the goddess of the moon,
goddess of the sun.
She was my love forever to come.
She'd shine like the morning
in the east where the sun came from.
She was like my everyday Valentine.
Love of a lifetime.
She'd whip away tears stop babies,
and adults from crying.
She was my love to forever shine.

She was the goddess the sun.
Marathons of life to win to won.
Cried out to stop the violence put down
the guns.

She was the goddess of the moon
couldn't wait for judgement day
prayed that the Lord would be coming back soon.

27. LOVELY

Lovely face.
Lovely place.
Lovely case.

28. Ever.....Lasting

Love everlasting.
Blessing to be casting.
Most gracious, satisfying.

29. ANY GIVING SEASON

Any giving season her aim was for pleasing.
Love breathing, breeding, believing.
Together no seperation or leaving.
Away from chaos fleeing.

30. LOVE TO

Love to live.
Love to give.
Love throughout timely sessions of years.
Love it is.
Love to live
Love to give.

UPCOMING NON-FICTION
BY ALAN HINES

IN MY EYES

1.

A lot of people always talk the things that what, and need in life, pertaining to wishing dreams of success, but only few out of an enormous percentage actually go out get it, do what it takes to live out dreams of success.

You even have those that complain about hard work and dedication, that is'nt intersted in hard work and dedication but yet and still desire, crave, yearn to be wealthy, successful, and in most cases it's never going to happen unless you inherit it, marry someone that is rich, and successful, or unless you hit the jackpot in the lottery; and the odds of any one of those things actually happen or extremely slim to none.

The things you want in life you got to go out and earn, and keep faith in the higher power that success will have it's turn to come to life within your life.

You got lawyers, and doctors that had to attend college for approximately eight years; but of course you got some lawyers that make more money than others depending on clientale, and on what branch of law they work in. As well as you got some doctors that make more money than others, but when it's all said and done majority of lawyers, and doctors make large percentage of finacial income, that's because they worked on the degrees for eight long years, and in the end it all paid off.....

I truly understand it's many distractions and some people lack resources but for those that really want to be successful you got to get out and earn it by all means, if you really want it.

Watch and see how those that didn't do anything with there life grow old and still be unfinancially stable contrary to those that worked hard and educated themselves turn out......

2.

T hose that's genuine with hearts of gold will constantly find themselves doing more giving and less receiving. Even those that's genuine and give without expecting nothing in return still may need help themselves later on within life; you'll see for yourself that those you went all out to help even giving your last wont help you not even in a small way after all did for them. Alot of people wont do the same things for you that you'll do for them if the shoe was on the other foot. Yet and still you gotta keep allowing your heart and mind to be pure, genuine even amongst strangers. Always reach out, and help others when you can with no secret motives or hidden agendas although some will misuse and most wont do the same for you, but keep doing what's best, helping the rest, and those that show you they are'nt worthy of such helpful treatment cut them short, but don't let the fakes hender your way of thinking and doing things.

3.

A t times you gotta let people be who they be. No matter how much you love them, and want them to change and do better, people can change and view things in different aspects only they're interested. But you still should put forth an effort to help those became better, and greater, but at a certain point if they're still not interested in changing you should'nt totally give up on them but face reality that people will be who they want to be; do the things they want to do. People will change only if they really want to.

4.

Y ou gotta take the bitter with the sweet. Life is'nt going to be always sweet. Even those with riches and fame often experience the bitterness of living within this earthly flesh within days of our lives. Sometimes the bitter times can turn out sweet. You can go through bitterness within a relationship or marriage that enabled you to be more appreciative of the new individual you'll date or even marry once the completion is over with your bitter companionships. Some people that's unfinancially unstable that's attending college for years struggling but once they're finished that's when the sweetness of life come shining through. Life is'nt always going to be sweet. You got to take the bitter with the sweet, you got to keep life moving, keep stepping making attempts to make things better than the last time.

5.

Loving From A Distance. You should always spread love like the wings of the Eagle; but in some cases you gotta show love from a distance. Maybe family members or friends, or the old neighborhood is fake or simply need good for, hinderous in your life someway, somehow preventing you from growth or simply taking from your happiness or impending happiness, or your self worth; you should still love certain people, places, or things, but only from a distance.

6.

No matter who you are we all need others from time to time. But yet and still we must try our best to be more self sufficient depending on our ownselves. Being the number one denomination within our own existence of salvation.

7.

Seek and find genuinest within the people you deal with. Although it's extremely difficult to find genuine people it is a few that still exist. Pay attention to all the things they do, draw off signs and symbols. When things are genuine you don't have to ask for or question it's automatically granted to you out of the genuinest concern, love from ones heart.

8.

You must expect the unexpected. You never know what may happen, or when something unexpecting may come to life within your life.

·

9.

You gotta deal with people for who they are. A theif is a theif; a cheater is a cheater; a snake is a snake. Some people get things twisted, they feel like a certain individual that is a family or friend and for whatever reason this family member or friend wouldn't do certain things to them for whatever reason. In reality a theif will steal something from you rather a family member or a friend. Some people meet people and started dating them when they was married to someone else, a cheater. Later on in life the one that was married divorced and married the one they was initially cheating on their spouse with. If you marry someone you met while he or she was married to someone else cheating on them what makes you think that person wont cheat on you?

10.

When dealing with people you gotta look at their entirety; rather it's a family member, a friendship or a relationship. You gotta look at them for who they are, and an each every level how you can deal with them. You can only deal with each and every person in your life to a certain extent. You gotta see where people at mentally, and see where they not at mentally. Rather it's a family, friend, or a lover you can expect people to think and do things on your level; the creator made us all different no two people are exactly the same, although alot of people have similarities to one another but not the same. You gotta see what people have to offer, as well as what you have to offer them. Many people get involved with relationship with people, maybe they were attractive, or they treated them good in the beginning; some didn't pay attention to the mishaps of that individual, others paid attention but overlooked some things. Later on down the road of the mishaps you may over look such things as you lover always simply flirting with others later on turned into he or she cheating with others; or he or she wasn't an all the way good parent to the kids he or she had prior to meeting you, and then once you get married and have kids you see the same things going on in your family, he or she still is'nt a good parent; I noticed quite a few women have that problem they'll see a guy they dating that have kids by someone else only being there for his kids partially or maybe not even at all and they'll have kids by him then complain that he's not a good father, when they already seen he wasn't a good father to his other kids. You may see someone always ditching work playing sick or whatever or simply not a good worker, and you may be a friend with a managers position, and help this ivdividual that's not a good worker or be missing alot of days and he she do the same thing once you get them hired at the company you work for. Although you may love people but you must understand you gotta deal with them on certain things, and on certain levels, it's impossible for you to deal with certain people on certain things on certain levels it's not going to work out.

11.

W ithin your existence of what it's formally called life you have to take a stand. Stand for something and don't fall for anything. You gotta stand for what you believe in to be right, because if you don't your beliefs will be held captive within you continious crying out for freedom. As much as we may dislike being not so nice at times you gotta let people know how you really feel inside. Even at times you gotta express to people how you really feel even over small issues; once you let people get away with small issues they'll attempt to do even more bigger things with the assumptions that they can get away with it. In history and possibly in the future people sacrificed their very own lives for what they believed in.

12.

He who has never sin should cast the first stone.

13.

Sometimes we complain about the things we don't have when we should be more appreciative of the things we do have.

14.

Keep working on it.
Keep rising.
Keep climbing.
Keep moving to the top.

15.

You can never actually feel the pain another person feel physically or mentally unless you've actually been through the exact same situation, and even then you can't still actually feel the exact pain that someone is experiencing, but you can somewhat feel their pain if you been through the same incident. Either way you must open up your heart and mind to help them through the pain.

16.

Y ou should love all, but trust none; the people that's close to you, like your family members or friends or a co-workers are the main ones that will do rotten stuff to you because they're the ones that are really close to you. Like the best bank robber will be someone that use to work at a bank, because they know the ways for a robber to attack, and be successful with the robbery. The same way a criminal or ex-criminal makes the best police;although those that can't pass a criminal background check will never actually be the police but the state and federal use them for confidential informants, to get close to other criminals to set them up for the authorities to catch them up doing unlawful things. Who's more better to get close to another criminal, a criminal is. And that's why you should never trust none especially those close to you.....

Love all, trust none.

17.

W alls of Silence. In life you create a mental as well physical wall of silence. You gotta sit back and listen to people pay attention, and analyze people, places, and things. Like when you first met an individual do less talking, more observation to see what type of individual your dealing with.

18.

Be grateful of the bad times; the bad times help you appreciate the good times even more. In some situatons of formats the bad times helps you become more self-sufficient with the ability to depend on yourself. The bad times allows us to see who are your real friends and who will be there in your time of need.